RACIAL PROFILING
CAUSES & CONSEQUENCES

Ronnie A. Dunn
Wornie Reed

Kendall Hunt
publishing company

Kendall Hunt
p u b l i s h i n g   c o m p a n y

www.kendallhunt.com
Send all inquiries to:
4050 Westmark Drive
Dubuque, IA 52004-1840

ISBN 978-0-7575-8686-6

Printed in the United States of America
10 9 8 7 6 5 4 3 2 1

CONTENTS

INTRODUCTION

Racial profiling is a phenomenon that has been around for many years; however, since the mid-1990s substantial attention has been given to racial profiling in general and "driving while black" (DWB) in particular. In fact, as of 2007 there had been over 200 court cases involving allegations of racial and ethnic profiling against law enforcement agencies in the United States.[1] Consequently, it is an issue of significant concern. This book investigates several aspects of this phenomenon.

Racial profiling can occur in a wide variety of instances and settings. It is a form of discrimination by which law enforcement uses a person's race or indicators of their cultural background as the primary reason to suspect that the individual has broken the law. The term "driving while black" arose from this practice, as African American drivers frequently complain that police officers pull them over for no other reason than the color of their skin and the stereotypes associated with their race.

Arab Americans and Muslim Americans became concerned with racial profiling following the terrorist attacks on September 11, 2001. Because the perpetrators of this crime were of Arab descent, Arabs in America complain that they are placed under intense scrutiny at airports and other locations. Although whites have committed domestic terrorist attacks, they have not been profiled in this manner.

While racial profiling can affect many aspects of the lives of minorities, we will focus on the DWB phenomenon. The Government Accountability Office defines the racial profiling of motorists as "using race as a key factor in deciding whether to make a traffic stop." Among the most frequently occurring incidences of racial profiling is traffic stops—for minor traffic violations, which often result in vehicle searches for contraband. That is the focus of this book, which includes several studies of traffic stops and assesses traffic stops from several perspectives.

One of the studies included is an analysis of reports from several states on data collected in traffic stops. These data indicate the race of the driver and the disposition of the traffic stop, i.e., race, search, and yield for contraband. This data was examined for evidence of racial discrimination. Several personal stories of DWB are also included in order to illuminate the pervasiveness of its occurrence.

A central part of this book is the report of studies of traffic ticketing in one city, Cleveland, Ohio. The approach we used in studying Cleveland's ticketing practices integrates research methods used in other studies to provide an enhanced estimate of the driving population within the particular geographic area being studied. Second, we analyze spatial and racial dynamics of the administration of justice as reflected in differential traffic enforcement practices used by the police in specific locations within the same municipal jurisdiction.

Third, we provide an analysis of the DWB issue from an institutional racism perspective rather than the traditional individual racist police officer paradigm in which the issue is generally discussed. As James M. Jones points out in distinguishing between these two forms of racism and their impact, while an individual may dislike a group of people because of their race, may call them derogatory names, give them a poor job rating, or refuse to hire them, an institutional practice or policy that systematically disadvantages a racial group and its members has consequences that are more widespread and reverberate and regenerate themselves for years.[2] By shifting the impetus of the discussion of racism from the individual to the institutional level, the personal burden of being labeled a "racist" and resistance to addressing the issue should be diminished.

We highlight the less obvious concomitant socioeconomic and legal ramifications of DWB such as the revocation of one's driver's license due to the accumulation of points for moving traffic violations and the various economic costs and hardships that stem from this loss of driving privileges, the possibility of multiple traffic infractions being added to a police record as was the case with Timothy Thomas, the young black man shot to death by Cincinnati police in 2001. We also discuss the implications of our findings. These include the following:

- The importance of looking at the policies, practices, and procedures in institutions.
- Racism is often in the policy and practice, not in the individual carrying out the policy.
- Systemic racism (against blacks or other minorities) can occur when the frontline actors are black or other minority themselves.

- Racially discriminatory practices can be shown to be attributes of institutions, instead of individuals.
- Considering the impact of institutional policies can facilitate meaningful discussions of remedies for racism.

STRUCTURE OF THE BOOK

The first chapter defines the problem, provides background information on DWB, discusses the literature on racial profiling, and legal rulings affecting it. In Chapter 2 we discuss cases of DWB. A study of traffic ticketing practices is reported in Chapter 3. Here we discuss approaches to defining the driving populations, and we analyze traffic ticketing patterns by race in Cleveland, including the use of a transportation planning model—the Gravity Model—to estimate the driving populations. In Chapter 4 we present the results of our study of stops, searches, and yields for contraband across several states. Chapter 5 describes the traffic surveys we conducted to assess actual speeding patterns by race, which we compared to the actual ticketing. Chapter 6 discusses institutional racism as an important perspective in assessing racial profiling. Chapter 7 discusses the consequences of racial profiling, e.g., felony records, unemployment, under-employment, poverty, etc. In Chapter 8, the Epilogue, Ronnie Dunn discusses the impact of the Cleveland study on public policy in that city and the attendant political reactions.

Please note that we tend to use the terms "black" and "African American" interchangeably. In most instances "black" would be the more appropriate term as distinctions are not being made between African Americans and other blacks.

NOTES

1. Antonovics, K. & B. G. Knight (February 2009). A New Look at Racial Profiling: Evidence from the Boston Police Department. *The Review of Economics and Statistics* 91(1): 163–177.
2. J. M. Jones, *Prejudice and Racism* (United States: McGraw-Hill Companies, 1997).

DRIVING WHILE BLACK

The issue of racial profiling has emerged as one of the most contentious and persistent social and political issues in the nation over the last 20 years. While the charge by minorities, particularly blacks, that they are singled out by law enforcement for disparate treatment is not a new phenomena as evidenced in the findings of the1968 Kerner Commission Report,[1] the increased surveillance of minorities in public spaces, particularly on the nation's roads and highways by police since the advent of the "War on Drugs" in the mid-1980s has brought the issue of racial profiling to the forefront of the public agenda. Although there is still a significant amount of disagreement and an ongoing debate among scholars, politicians, law enforcement officials, and advocates on both sides of this issue as to whether law enforcement engage in singling out blacks and other minorities for differential treatment and law enforcement practices, particularly in traffic enforcement, a growing number of states and local jurisdictions have begun to collect and analyze racial demographic data in traffic enforcement to address the issue.

Prior to the terrorist attacks of 9/11, the term *racial profiling* most commonly referred to the targeting and stopping of black motorists by police on the pretense of some traffic violation. While racial profiling, or "DWB" (driving while black), the phrase coined by blacks and adopted by the media to refer to such practices, is a relatively new term, the actions that define it are not. It describes the use of pretextual traffic stops which are traffic stops of motorists, particularly minorities, by law enforcement officers under the guise of a minor traffic violation as justification to search their vehicles and/or persons for drugs, guns, and other forms of contraband.[2] The most egregious consequences of such traffic stops are those incidents involving the use of force by police, which sometimes result in the death of a motorist at the hands of the police.[3] At the very least, this practice brings into question the violation of members of these minority groups' constitutional protections under the Fourth and Fourteenth Amendments against "unreasonable search and seizure without probable cause" and providing "equal protection under the law," and predisposes them to being disproportionately ticketed in relation to their percentage of the driving population.[4]

Since the advent of the War on Drugs in the 1980s, pretextual stops have been increasingly used as a crime-fighting technique by law enforcement agencies throughout the country.[5] Law enforcement officials base their defense of this practice on the argument that "blacks commit a disproportionate number of crimes, and are particularly involved in drug trafficking."[6] Therefore, they contend, using race as a proxy for criminality is a justified and valid law enforcement practice.[7]

The premise of blacks' excessive involvement in drug trafficking is based, in part, on statistics that suggest African Americans are disproportionately involved in crime, particularly drug-related crimes. African Americans constitute 12.3 percent of the U.S. population yet represent 39 percent of all persons incarcerated in jails[8] and 41 percent of the nation's prison population.[9] Recent studies have shown that only 61 percent of this differential incarceration of blacks can be attributed to disproportionate engagement in criminal behavior. Consequently, the other 39 percent must be attributed to disparities in criminal justice processing. These disparities are quite evident in processing of drug offenses. Blacks are 14 percent of drug users[10] and 14 percent of drug sellers[11]; however, they are 34 percent of persons arrested for drug offenses, 53 percent of drug convictions, and 63 percent of all drug offenders admitted to state prisons.[12]

The opponents of the use of racial profiling by law enforcement argue that such figures highlight the racial bias within the criminal justice system and the War on Drugs' criminalization of African Americans, particularly black males. They suggest that law enforcement agencies have disproportionately targeted street-level drug dealers and drug addicts in America's black and brown inner cities, instead of going after the middle- and top-level drug traffickers, who are responsible for distribution channels that funnel drugs to the street-level dealers, or the white-suburban majority of the drug-abusing population.

BACKGROUND

Charges of abuse and unfair treatment of blacks at the hands of the police in America have long been voiced by blacks, and was cited by the Kerner Commission Report as one of the primary causes leading to the urban riots of the late 1960s. The Report found that these incidences of abuse against blacks by police often resulted from a traffic stop.[13] In spite of the Report's findings and its recommendations to address the dehumanizing police violation of the civil and human rights of persons in America's black ghettoes, this social issue has for the most part, remained dormant in the American consciousness and has not been addressed in any substantive manner within the public agenda. Joe Feagin traces this history of police violence against blacks back to after the Civil War when private and police violence was used "to create and maintain the system of enforced segregation" that resulted from white fears of the newly freed black Americans.[14] The legacy of police abuse has become an unfortunate yet enduring fact of life for most African Americans and other people of color.[15] Not until the occurrence of an increasing number of highly publicized cases of police abuse and deadly use of force against unarmed black males since the early 1990s, viz., those of Rodney King in Los Angeles, Johnny Gammage in Pittsburgh, Abner Louima and Amadou Diallo in New York City, and Timothy Thomas and Nathaniel Jones in Cincinnati, has the issue begun to receive heightened public scrutiny and come to the forefront of the public agenda. Each of the aforementioned cases, with the exception of King and Louima, resulted in the beating or shooting death of the unarmed, black victim with police officers contending that they feared for their lives.

The intense media attention created by these cases combined with the continual reports of prominent African Americans, such as NAACP President Kwesi Mfume, former Congressman Harold E. Ford Jr., (D-TN), attorney Johnnie Cochran, actors Blair Underwood and Wesley Snipes, and Pro Football Hall of Fame star Marcus Allen being the target of DWB has lead to a concerted effort by black leaders, the American Civil Liberties Union (ACLU), and black communities throughout the country. These elements have coalesced to compel lawmakers in all levels of government, and law enforcement agencies, to address this matter.

Congressman John Conyers (D-MI) introduced the Traffic Stops Statistics Study Act (H.R. 118) before the U.S. House of Representatives in 1998 to address racial profiling. If passed, this legislation would require law enforcement agencies to collect and maintain records of each driver's race, whether a search was conducted, and if a ticket was given on each traffic stop made. While a twin resolution (S.821) was introduced in the Senate by Senators Frank Lautenberg (D-NJ) and Russell Feingold (D-WI) in 1999, and both pieces of legislation have been reintroduced in each subsequent session of Congress, the legislation has yet to pass in both Houses of Congress. This legislation would provide the U.S. Attorney General's office with the necessary quantitative data to adequately document patterns of police abuse and neglect of which African Americans have continually provided anecdotal reports for years.[16] Armed with the appropriate empirical evidence the U.S. Justice Department has the authority to file civil legal proceedings to eradicate "patterns or practices of police misconduct" under "The Violent Crime Control and Law Enforcement Act of 1994," and "The Safe Streets Act of 1968," where warranted.

The ACLU's national campaign calls upon the Justice Department, law enforcement officials, and federal, state, and local legislators to join a comprehensive, five-part battle to eliminate the practice of racial profiling. This plan calls for ending the use of pretextual stops, passage of the Traffic Stops Statistics Study Act, passing legislation on traffic stops in every state, the Justice Department ensuring that racial profiling is not used in federally funded drug interdiction programs, and the 50 largest U.S. cities agreeing to voluntarily collect traffic stop data.[17]

Lawsuits have been filed on behalf of DWB victims in several states. Maryland paid damages in a class action suit after a pattern of state police harassing black motorists along Interstate Highway-95 was discovered. Former New Jersey Governor Christine Todd Whitman fired then-state police superintendent, Carl Williams, for defending the practice of racial profiling. Williams's comment that "the drug problem is mostly cocaine and marijuana . . . it is most likely minorities that are involved with that"[18] was made in response to a study conducted by Professor John Lamberth of Temple University, which found that whites were 75 percent of the motorists and traffic violators along a stretch of I-95 running through New Jersey, yet 80 percent of the vehicles stopped and searched belonged to minorities.[19]

The Justice Department has entered consent decree agreements with several municipal law enforcement agencies where patterns of police misconduct and racial bias were found including the Pittsburgh Police Department, and the Steubenville and Cincinnati Police Departments in Ohio. As these and other efforts throughout the country aimed at addressing racial profiling or DWB were gaining momentum, the September 11th bombing of the World Trade Center shifted the focus of racial profiling away from issues pertaining to blacks and Hispanics to people of Arab or Middle Eastern decent. The issue of targeting persons perceived as being potential terrorists on American soil and against American interests abroad not only expanded the discussion of racial profiling: It took precedence over the issue of DWB on the public agenda. This study refocuses on the pre-9/11 issue of the racial profiling of blacks, in particular, the issue of Driving While Black.

A study of racial profiling in the state of Ohio commissioned by the Ohio state legislature and conducted by Harris[20] found patterns of racial disparities in the traffic ticket data for four of the state's five largest municipalities.[21] Cleveland is the second largest city in Ohio and the third most racially segregated city in the nation.[22] While the Cleveland Police Department began voluntarily collecting racial data on traffic tickets in 1999, these data were not available for analysis at the time of Harris's study. However, acting upon reports of racist organizations and activities within the Cleveland Police Department from trusted sources within the police force, then Mayor Michael R. White initiated an investigation of the department for evidence of organized racist activity in the summer of 2000. While the investigation concluded that there was no verifiable evidence of racist organizations operating within the police department, an internal memorandum included in the report from the deputy chief of operations to the chief of police reported that the Cleveland Police Department did engage in racial profiling against blacks in the city.[23] Although the memorandum included details on the manner in which the department engaged in this practice and provided statistics supporting this contention, this aspect of the report was not discussed in the local media's final reports on the investigation's findings.

As noted, African Americans are disproportionately represented at every stage along the punitive continuum within the nation's criminal justice system, from detainment to incarceration. Blacks are arrested, prosecuted, convicted, and incarcerated at rates out of proportion with the 12.3 percent of the population they represent, and in comparison to whites. The primary question debated among scholars is whether these disparities are the result of racial discrimination within the criminal justice system.

While scholars disagree about the root causes of the disparities between blacks and whites involved in the criminal justice system, there is little disagreement about the magnitude of the problem. Some describe the problem in terms of a national crisis as African Americans represent 40 percent of the nation's jail and prison population.[24] One in every eight black males in their 20s is in prison or jail on any given day.[25] And black males have a 32 percent chance of serving time in prison at some point in their lives and Hispanic males have a 17 percent chance, compared to 6 percent for whites.[26]

Schrantz and McElroy suggest that such disparities, which are "rarely a result of clear-cut decisions to provide unfair treatment, threaten to produce in communities in every city and state an unhealthy and counterproductive distrust of the criminal justice system."[27] Elijah Anderson describes this erosion of trust in the criminal justice system within the black ghetto as a loss of faith in civil law, which he argues further contributes to the decay of the moral fabric in these communities.[28]

CONCEPTUAL FRAMEWORK

There are two primary perspectives that form the theoretical basis for examining the racial disparities within the criminal justice system and the related issues of racial profiling and DWB: Consensus Theory and Conflict Theory.

Consensus Theory

Consensus theory is the principal theoretical framework that holds that equality is an essential value within the criminal justice system, and societal sanctions are imposed objectively on those who break the law. In general, this theory purports that sanctions are applied to behavior irrespective of sociodemographic factors such as the race and socioeconomic characteristics of the offender. Implicit in consensus theory's postulate is the belief that social control sanctions are administered objectively and explicit in many of its proponents' arguments, is the presupposition that the disproportionate punitive involvement of minorities in the criminal justice system is the result of their increased involvement in criminal behavior not racial discrimination.[29] Although most consensus theorists support this general hypothesis there are variations within the tradition.

One of the most ardent proponents of the consensus theory tradition within criminology and the "No Discrimination Thesis"(NDT) is William Wilbanks.[30] Wilbanks asserts that the perception of the criminal justice system as racist is "a myth." Wilbanks writes that the system is not characterized by racial prejudice or discrimination against blacks. He declares that, "at every point from arrest to parole there is little or no evidence of an overall racial effect, in that the percentage outcomes of blacks and whites are not very different."

To support his argument, Wilbanks uses 1980 arrest and incarceration data from California and Pennsylvania to analyze the reported eight-to-one difference between the incarceration rates for blacks and whites. Wilbanks reported a 20 percent increase in the black-to-white gap from arrest to incarceration in California compared to a 9 percent decrease in the black-to-white gap from arrest to incarceration in Pennsylvania. From this, he concludes that "overall, it would appear that the black/white gap does not increase from arrest to prison . . . thus, there is no evidence overall that black offenders processed by the criminal justice system fare worse than white offenders."[31]

Wilbanks inexplicably dismisses the disproportionate incarceration rate that exists for blacks in California by presenting data from Pennsylvania where, although a decrease in the black/white gap from arrest to incarceration was noted, a disproportion does exist nonetheless. He enigmatically suggests that the decrease in Pennsylvania offsets any disparities that exist between blacks and whites from arrest to incarceration in the two states. Unlike Albert Blumstein, who in his studies on black-to-white arrests and incarceration rates identified the disproportionate arrest-to-incarceration rates found as plausibly reflecting discrimination in the criminal justice system, Wilbanks suggests that what discrimination does exist in the system comes in the form of "breaks" given by decision makers. Conceding that there is evidence that some individual decision makers (e.g., police officers, judges) are more likely to give "breaks" to whites than blacks, he goes on to contend that there is an equal tendency for other individual decision makers to favor blacks over whites. Following the same rationale that he used in comparing the arrest to incarceration data from California and Pennsylvania, Wilbanks asserts that a "canceling-out effect" occurs within the criminal justice system as an equal number of these individual decision makers give whites a "break" as those favoring blacks. This, he concludes, results in studies that find "no overall racial effect."

Wilbanks states that the vast majority of blacks believe that the police and courts discriminate against blacks, while the majority of whites deny this claim. He adds that a sizeable minority of whites even believe that the criminal justice system actually has a pro-black bias and "leans over backward" to appease blacks in response to charges of racism from the black community and the media.[32]

Other research supporting consensus theory indicates that criminal activity and the seriousness of the offense are stronger predictors of the black-to-white arrest disparities than social, economic, cultural or demographic variables and are evidence of some of the impartial application of sanctions within the criminal justice system.[33] The work of Blumstein is a frequently cited example of research supporting this position within consensus theory. In an update to his study of the racial disproportionality between blacks and whites in U.S. prisons, Blumstein compared 1970s crime statistics on arrest[34] and imprisonment to figures from the 1980s.[35] In the earlier study Blumstein found that roughly 80 percent of the racial disproportionality in prisons was accounted for by the differential involvement of blacks in arrests for serious crimes such as murder and robbery, which generally lead to incarceration.[36] The latter study revealed an increase in the unexplained disproportionality as 76 percent of the disparity in imprisonment could be explained by differential arrest data. Blumstein states that while racial discrimination is part of the unexplained racial disproportionality found in the studies (20 percent and 24 percent respectively), its precise measure could not be determined. He suggests that discrimination can account for all or none of this residual disproportionality, which could also include other legitimate factors that can contribute to incarceration, such as prior arrest record and employment status.[37]

With the exception of drug crimes, the aggregate black-to-white disproportionality incarceration rate for serious crimes remained relatively constant in both studies.[38] What increased disproportionality was found in the later study was due to a striking increase in the number of blacks arrested and imprisoned on drug charges in the 1980s. Alarmed by this increased disproportionality associated with drug crimes Blumstein surmises that:

> **Drug arrests are not necessarily indicative of offending patterns and probably are associated with over-arresting of blacks compared to whites. These facts, combined with the high prevalence of young black males under control of the criminal justice system, must raise serious questions about the degree to which the policy associated with the drug war has significantly exacerbated the racial disproportionality in prisons.[39]**

In essence, Blumstein's studies found that while black involvement in serious crimes would account for a significant portion of the disproportionality in incarceration, racial discrimination could account for some of the unexplained residual disproportionality, the exact amount of which is unknown.

Michael Tonry[40] contends that although some scholars argue that the racial disparities in incarceration result from racial bias operating at every criminal justice stage from arrest to parole release, and while no one denies that there is bias in the system, many scholars and most officials believe that racial disproportions result largely from different racial patterns of criminality and that bias is a relatively small, though immensely important, part of the problem.[41]

In essence, Blumstein, Tonry, and Wilbanks reflect different perspectives within the consensus theory tradition on whether racial discrimination exists within the criminal justice system. Blumstein and Tonry represent a more liberal view within consensus theory in that they acknowledge that some of the difference in the black-to-white incarceration rates can possibly be attributed to some degree of racial discrimination within the criminal justice system, although thought to be minimal.[42] Wilbanks on the other hand, epitomizes the more extreme or conservative view within the consensus theory tradition, which holds that systemic racial discrimination does not exist within the criminal justice system and any racial differences in black-to-white incarceration rates are the result of blacks' increased involvement in crime.[43]

Conflict Theory

Conflict theory is the antithesis of consensus theory and argues that the disparities and inequalities between social groups within the criminal justice system are the result of discrimination. Conflict theorists such as Coramae Richey Mann[44] are critical of consensus theory arguments such as Wilbanks' that dismiss or downplay the significance of evidence of racial bias in the criminal justice system as she argues, "even a single verified case of unequal sentencing because of racial status serves to illuminate flaws in the criminal justice system, and indeed ample research demonstrates that there are thousands of such cases."

In the original conceptualization of conflict theory proponents used a social class perspective[45] to explain that the disparities faced by minorities are foundational and essential to the maintenance of the social order, while others[46] have adapted a racial/ethnic based perspective of conflict theory to account for the inequalities experienced by minorities within the criminal justice system, in particular.[47]

Arguing from a race-based orientation of conflict theory, Hawkins asserts that "non-whites will receive more severe punishment than whites for all crimes, under all conditions, and at similar levels of disproportion over time."[48] Richey Mann adds that, "racial discrimination is endemic to, ingrained in, and permeates the American criminal justice system."[49]

According to Cureton, conflict theory also maintains that legal sanctions are applied to those groups that are perceived as a threat to the status and interests of the elite. He puts forth that minorities pose a threat to the social and political order of elites due to minority's subordinate status, conduct, jealousy and envy, suspicion, and cultural or racial differences. These groups are said to present a greater threat when they are concentrated in a geographical area, in that this maximizes the probability of concerted action. From this, Cureton says, the amount of police presence and control in certain jurisdictions is positively correlated with the geographic concentration and density of members of the perceived threat group within the jurisdiction.[50]

Research conducted by Bridges et al.[51] provides empirical evidence to support Cureton's argument relating the level of police presence in a particular area with the concentration of members of a perceived threat group (e.g., minorities, and/or the poor) within the area. This research also contradicts Blumstein's assertions that arrests for the differential levels of serious and violent crimes committed account for the majority of the disproportionality found in the imprisonment rates for blacks and whites.

Bridges et al. used county-level measures of crime and arrest rates, social structure, and the criminal justice system to determine their effect on differential imprisonment rates between whites and nonwhites in Washington State. These authors constructed variables on county crime and arrest rates including serious and violent crimes, the workload of county courts, the amount of urbanization, the degree of white/nonwhite economic inequality, and the percentage of the minority population within each county to measure the impact of crime and the criminal justice system on white and minority incarceration rates.

Consistent with Cureton's assertion and conflict theory, this study found the percentage of the population that was minority was more strongly related to minority imprisonment rates than to white imprisonment rates in that minority imprisonment rates increased significantly as the size of the minority population increased, while there was no effect on the white imprisonment rates. And contradicting consensus theory and Blumstein's findings Bridges et al. state, "the levels of violent crime and arrest rates have surprisingly limited influences on rates of imprisonment. Although the effect is statistically significant in one instance—the nonwhite arrest rate—other aspects of community social structure contribute much more to variation in imprisonment."[52]

This study found the minority population percentage had a much greater effect on minority incarceration rates than the indirect effects of the violent crime rate or the white and nonwhite arrest rates. Also at odds with the findings of previous studies, which claim that the bureaucratization of the courts and criminal justice systems, characteristic of those found in urban areas, reduces the likelihood that minorities will be more severely punished for crimes, this study found that "urbanization actually increases the non-white imprisonment rate." Thus, Bridges et al. conclude that as the minority population increases, particularly in areas where minorities are segregated and crime is more intense, there is a heightened sense that minorities pose a threat to the social order, and in turn, law enforcement officials implement informal strategies of social control that have racially disparate outcomes.[53]

Also arguing within the conflict theory tradition or what is referred to by criminologists as the "Discrimination Thesis" (DT), Georges-Abeyie uses the concept of "petit apartheid" to describe what he views as "a range of punitively discriminatory, discretionary acts" within the criminal justice system.

According to Georges-Abeyie, this range of acts which consists of, but is not limited to, "the excessive and unnecessary stops, searches and questioning by police; condescending judges; narrow instructions by judges to juries; and less stringent standards of evidence used in convictions of minorities," represents the day-to-day discrimination against blacks and other ethnic minorities.[54] He, in concurrence with Cureton and Bridges et al., asserts that patterns of discriminatory practices occur within areas characterized by expanding "residential spatial segregation," or "specific ecological zones of the alleged ghetto, slum-ghetto, or non-ghetto," which form the center of discriminatory policing, and the prominence of multifaceted and changing "spatial dynamics."[55]

Similar to the findings cited above, the results of other studies analyzing whether the disproportionate representation of blacks in the criminal justice system is the result of racial discrimination have been mixed, with compelling research and arguments supporting both consensus theory[56] and conflict theory.[57] As Richey Mann states, "the few available studies of this issue offer support to both sides of the question."[58] However, although compelling evidence and arguments are presented by both sides in this debate, we concur with the conflict theorists who contend that much of the racial disparities found in criminal justice statistics are a reflection of the policing practices and deployment patterns that often are concentrated in areas with considerable minority populations.[59] The heightened police presence and surveillance prevalent in many minority communities can subject residents to increased contacts with the police, which ultimately could result in their involvement with the criminal justice system. Thus, a closer look needs to be taken at the relations between the police and citizens of such communities. This will be done by first looking at the historical relationship between the black community and the police and then looking at contemporary encounters between blacks and the police.

RELATIONSHIP BETWEEN BLACK COMMUNITIES AND THE POLICE

The use of race and space as the basis for the disparate treatment of blacks has been a pernicious and persistent problem throughout American history. From slavery, through the legalized segregation of the Jim Crow Era, to the present, race has been used as a means of social control against blacks.[60]

As Feagin states, "the color and cultural differences of Africans (blacks) made them easier for whites to identify for purposes of enslavement and control" during slavery.[61] According to Wintersmith, legislation known as Slave Codes or Black Codes were enacted in the independent states and commonwealths following the Revolutionary War to institutionalize and legalize the customs and practices on which slavery rested prior to the founding of the nation.[62]

It was through the enforcement of these Black Codes that the roots of the relationship between the black community and the police were established, argues Wintersmith. He cites South Carolina legislation enacted in 1690 as establishing a policing function by requiring "all persons under penalty of forty shillings to arrest and chastise any slave out of his home plantation without a proper ticket." He asserts that few counties in the slave states did not have a local police patrol known as "patterollers" whose primary responsibility was to contain the slaves and enforce the Black Codes. According to Wintersmith, these patterollers were usually poor, young whites, that did not own slaves but "whose favorite sport was Negro catching, watching, whipping, and intimidating."[63]

After the end of slavery with the passage of the 13th and 14th Amendments the Black Codes were subsumed under Jim Crow and the legal doctrine of "separate but equal" which circumscribed black life in America from the end of Reconstruction in 1877 until the Supreme Court ruling in *Brown v. Topeka Board of Education* (1954) and passage of the 1960's Civil Rights legislation.[64] Feagin cites the historical role of white police officers as the principal agents of the violent repression of black Americans, particularly through the Jim Crow era. According to Feagin, "in the years 1920–1932 substantially more than half of all African Americans killed by whites were killed by police officers," and police were implicated in the 6,000 lynchings of black men and women that were recorded between the 1870s and the 1960s.[65]

In spite of the legal rulings finding racial segregation and discrimination unconstitutional and federal legislation against these practices, blacks continued to experience both, particularly in the black ghettoes of America's northern cities where they had become segregated since the second wave of the Great Migration following WWII. The federal government was complicit in helping to create the contemporary racial housing patterns known as "chocolate cities and vanilla suburbs" found in cities such as Cleveland, by facilitating "white flight" to the suburbs through federally funded programs such as Federal Housing Administration (FHA) and GI loans, and the development of the interstate highway system, in the midst of the booming, post-WWII economy.[66]

Not only were these programs and opportunities not available to most blacks, but the federal government also enacted Urban Renewal during this same period. This program, which was intended to be a slum clearance program, became known as "Negro Removal." Once low-income housing units were cleared in black communities, replacement housing was often never built. Between 1950 and 1960 approximately 126,000 housing units were destroyed, 101,000 of which were substandard. It is estimated that only 28,000 housing units were built during this period, the majority of which were high-rent apartments.[67] This forced displaced families into other segregated inner-city communities. Urban renewal only further perpetuated the racial segregation of the nation's central cities and suburbs and the polarization of their black and white populations.

These federal policies coupled with the racially discriminatory practices of "blockbusting," "racial steering," and the use of "racial covenants" by the real estate industry along with "redlining" by the banking industry coalesced to solidify the boundaries of the black ghettoes. In the city of Cleveland, the boundaries of the ghetto had come to confine the majority of the city's black population to the Central neighborhood by the 1930s,[68] but has since expanded to encompass numerous neighborhoods on the city's predominately black East Side including the Fairfax and Hough neighborhoods as indicated by the concentrated poverty in these neighborhoods referred to in Chapter 3.

The oppressive living conditions within black ghettoes nationwide led to a series of riots in cities throughout the country during the summer of 1966, including Hough in Cleveland. Feagin reports that an analysis of riots in black communities between 1943 and 1972 indicates that the immediate precipitating event of many uprisings was the killing or harassment of black men by white police officers. And as noted in Chapter 1, the Kerner Commission Report stated that, "virtually every urban rebellion that took place during the sixties was immediately preceded by police-black-citizen confrontations."[69]

CITIZEN ENCOUNTERS WITH POLICE

A review of the literature on encounters between blacks, the police, and the criminal justice system reveals the contemporary issue of "driving while black." The police represent the gatekeepers or the centurions of the criminal justice system. They are usually the first and the most frequent contact that the average citizen has with the criminal justice system.[70] For most citizens, these contacts with police come in the form of traffic stops. A Bureau of Justice Statistics survey of citizens 16 years of age and older on their encounters with police, found that roughly 21 percent of the public had at least one direct, face-to-face contact with a police officer in 1999. Motor vehicle stops were the most frequent reason for contact between the public and police, accounting for 52 percent of such encounters. Citizens calling to report crime was the next most prevalent reason, constituting 20 percent of all contacts with police.[71]

A key determinant in the outcome of these initial contacts between individuals and the police is "police discretion," which is defined as the "selective enforcement of the law by duly authorized police agents." Discretion is defined as "the authority conferred by law to act in certain conditions or situations in accordance with an official's or agency's own considered conscience or judgment."[72]

As "street-level" administrators of justice, police hold a unique and powerful position in the criminal justice system. They exercise wide discretionary control over who is stopped, detained, arrested, and ultimately comes under the control of the criminal justice system or is diverted from the system at this initial point of entry.[73] Unlike the decisions made by other agents of the criminal justice system such as prosecutors and judges, the "street-level" justice administered by police more often than not occurs outside of the realm of public knowledge, scrutiny, and oversight. This power of discretion as exercised by police is known as low-visibility decision making. Due to the low visibility of police discretion in this context, it is suggested that discretion can sometimes deteriorate into discrimination, violence, and other forms of abuse by the police.[74] In essence, discretion allows the police to determine to whom and under what circumstances the law is applied.

LEGAL RULINGS RELATED TO RACIAL PROFILING AND DWB

Germane to the discussion of police discretion as it relates to racial profiling and DWB is the legal precedence established by the U.S. Supreme Court in its 1968 ruling in *Terry v. Ohio*. This precedent-setting case stemmed from a citizen and police encounter, which took place on a downtown Cleveland street in 1963. On October 31, 1963, while patrolling the downtown streets, Officer Martin McFadden, a white Cleveland police officer, observed two black men, John Terry and Richard Chilton, on the corner of E. 14th and Euclid Avenue. McFadden watched the men for 10 minutes as they took turns walking back and forth, looking in store windows. When later asked during testimony what drew his attention to Terry and Chilton, McFadden stated, "well to tell you the truth, I didn't like them." Suspecting them of "casing a job, a stick-up," McFadden stopped the men along with Carl Katz, a white male he had seen Terry and Chilton conversing with, identified himself as a police officer, and proceeded to frisk the trio. Both Terry and Chilton had loaded guns and were arrested and convicted of carrying concealed weapons.[75]

Terry appealed his case, arguing that his Fourth Amendment right against "unreasonable search and seizure" had been violated. The U.S. Supreme Court ruled against Terry and used its decision to try to establish the legal parameters governing the use of "stop and frisk" procedures by the police to guard against "unreasonable search and seizure" and to circumscribe police discretion in determining when there is "probable cause" to believe that a crime for which an arrest can be made has occurred.[76]

Although the Court upheld the lower court's ruling in *Terry v. Ohio*, some fundamental arguments related to the issue of racial profiling were raised during the Supreme Court hearings. As former Congressman Louis Stokes, then counsel for the plaintiff (Terry), argued in questioning the state's request of the Court to interpret an officer's reasonable suspicion as probable cause:

> **We look at the hundreds of people walking the street by the day, because a police officer finds himself observing a situation where he says, as he did in this case, "Well, to tell you the truth, I just didn't like them and then I began watching them." And then the fact that he wants to go further—and at that point, I think we're subjecting all of the people who have this inviolate right of privacy, to this type of activity on the public streets throughout our nation.[77]**

While this argument relates specifically to the issue of police discretion, which is of less significance in analyzing the issue of racial profiling or racially biased law enforcement practices from an institutional racism perspective, it speaks to the broad discretion given to the law enforcement institution and its agents to subject virtually any citizen in public space to detainment, search, and possibly arrest based on a suspicion, intuition, or even personal prejudice toward certain groups.

The 1996 U.S. Supreme Court decision *Whren v. United States* ruled that any traffic offense committed by a driver was a legitimate legal basis for a stop.[78] This widened police officer discretion in making traffic stops. Prior to *Whren*, officers needed "probable cause" about suspicion of illegal activity to make a traffic stop. The *Whren* decision permitted officers to make pretextual stops, perhaps based on very minor traffic infractions, that could put them in a position to better detect whether drug activity is taking place or not. Thus *Whren* supported the broad discretion exercised by law enforcement in making traffic stops and essentially enabled law enforcement officers to make traffic stops based on subjective, or even discriminatory motivation.

In his assessment of the impact of the lower courts' interpretations of *Terry v. Ohio* since the ruling was handed down, Harris argues that in spite of the Court's requirement that police "base their reasonable suspicion on specific facts involving the particular person under observation . . . the lower courts have gradually but unmistakably eroded the force of these words." He contends that the lower courts have established a criterion that allows police to conduct stop and frisk "when individuals fit into one or two categories of entirely innocent activity: simply being in a high crime area or exhibiting a desire to avoid the police or both." Harris's primary criticism of this reduced legal standard is "not that these cases allow police to stop and frisk based on whether individual behavior falls into one of these categories, but rather that these categories are so broad that they are far too likely to result in innocent people being stopped and frisked, and too unlikely to include the guilty."[79] In concurrence with Stokes's earlier argument Harris suggests that "soon given the direction of the law, this system of categorical rules will allow police to stop and frisk almost anyone they want, with minimal interference from the courts."[80] Harris concludes that African Americans and other minority groups will disproportionately shoulder this burden given that they overwhelmingly tend to live in "high crime areas" and may have legitimate reasons to want to avoid having contact with the police such as prior experiences of harassment, unjustified detentions and searches, or even physical abuse at the hands of the police.[81]

The first of these categories described by Harris, the stopping of individuals within high crime areas, is of particular interest in relation to the locational aspects of the differential law enforcement practices.

SELECTIVE/DIFFERENTIAL LAW ENFORCEMENT, AND SPATIAL PROFILING

As Smith and Visher[82] point out, while police have a legal mandate to enforce the law uniformly, most scholars agree that selective enforcement is customary in contemporary police work. Kenneth Culp Davis contends that all American police departments adhere to a deeply entrenched system that combines selective enforcement with the pretense of full enforcement of the law.[83] This raises the critical issue of under what criterion is the law being applied. One school of thought suggests that patterns of selective enforcement will mirror the social stratification within society, thereby most adversely affecting members of socially disadvantaged groups such as blacks and the poor. The situation for blacks would be further exacerbated in that blacks are disproportionately represented among the poor.[84] As Schrantz and McElroy explain, whether one acquires a criminal record is clearly in part related to the level of criminal activity, but it is also a function of race, geographic location and other factors. Georges-Abeyie contends that discriminatory policing practices are manifested in "specific ecological zones." These ecological zones, which are neighborhoods that have or are undergoing racial/ethnic transformation, are comparable to the transition zones in the Chicago School's urban ecology, Concentric Zone Model.[85] These neighborhoods or transition zones in the

Chicago School model were also designated as "high crime areas," those in which minorities are likely to be subjected to the type of police practices described by Harris and Stokes.

We use the concept "spatial profiling" to characterize the differential law enforcement practices that these scholars suggest police employ in specific geographic areas, distinguished primarily by the race of the population of particular communities. This concept embodies aspects of Michel Foucault's analysis of the "carceral system" and its surveillance of a designated "dangerous" or "criminal class" of the urban population as a social control mechanism. Foucault's account of the penalty in the late 18th century highlights a shift in the impetus of punishment from the "body of the condemned" toward "a more finely tuned justice, towards a closer mapping of the social body."[86] Foucault describes the attendant characteristics of the carceral system's penality as:

> **A way of handling illegalities, of laying down the limits of tolerance, of giving free rein to some, of putting pressure on others, of excluding a particular section, of making another useful, of neutralizing certain individuals and of profiting from others . . . penalty does not simply "check" illegalities; it "differentiates" them, it provides them with a general "economy" . . . if one can speak of justice, it is not only because the law itself or the way of applying it serves the interest of a class, it is also because the differential administration of illegalities through the mediation of penalty forms part of those mechanisms of domination.**[87]

Also related to this concept of "spatial profiling" and Foucault's "carceral system" is the work of Neil Websdale and Loïc Wacquant. Websdale refers to the carceral system as the "criminal justice juggernaut," which he describes as "that growing web of prisons, jails, law enforcement, probation, and parole that regulates the lives of so many among the poor, particularly black people." He views recent forms of saturation law enforcement, which includes community policing, "as the lead filter for the juggernaut, providing it with new bodies, new clientele, new cases, new sources of funding, and allegedly, new credibility." He describes the function of this criminal justice juggernaut as the "overall state management of surplus populations" consisting of the unemployed, the underemployed, the homeless, and the otherwise urban disenchanted. Websdale contends that regulating a permanent postindustrial underclass requires a special punitive energy and that the criminal justice juggernaut and its community policing function provide this energy.[88]

Wacquant uses a historical perspective to illustrate the link between the present-day carceral system with its black hyper-incarceration and slavery. He argues that the task of defining, confining, and controlling African Americans in the United States has been successively shouldered by four "peculiar institutions": slavery, the Jim Crow system, the urban ghetto, and the novel organizational compound formed by the vestiges of the ghetto and the expanding carceral system. Wacquant views the role of these institutions as serving the dual purposes of "labor extraction and social ostracization," with each successive institution carrying out these objectives throughout the changing socioeconomic context of the nation's history.[89]

Wacquant contends that the erosion of the indigenous black institutions in place in the black ghettos by the 1950s have left a vacuum that has been filled by state bureaucracies of social control: welfare/workfare programs; public housing authorities; public health and public school systems; and the police, courts and the on-the-ground extensions of the penal system, i.e. probation officers, and parole agents. He suggests that these social control appendages of the penal system "extend the mesh of state surveillance and capture deep into the hyper-ghetto."[90]

What Websdale and Wacquant are referring to is the manner in which the criminal justice juggernaut or carceral system is a self-perpetuating system that justifies its existence through its ability to define as criminal and take in an ever-increasing number of subjects. The majority of these subjects are invariably black given the ubiquitous police presence and surveillance found in predominately black inner-city communities and ghettoes.

In essence, the concept of "spatial profiling" can be understood to represent the differential law enforcement practices used by police in particular geographical areas, where two seemingly different standards of law enforcement appear to be in effect for persons of different racial groups. It is a social control measure used by law enforcement that, intentionally or unintentionally, surveils and circumscribes the actions and movement of members of certain racial/ethnic groups when functioning within public space. This concept differs from racial profiling in that it pertains to the heightened visibility given minorities by law enforcement not only in areas where they are deemed "out of place" or are a numerical minority, but also even in their own communities where they are the majority, yet are subjected to increased scrutiny in relation to that received by non-minorities operating within the same public space.

We borrow from Foucault's analysis of "spaces of constructed visibility" to illustrate whether the traffic ticketing practices or "technologies" used by the police department in Cleveland systematically targets African Americans within the city for a disproportionate share of traffic violations, thereby constituting institutional racism.[91] See Chapter 3. Such an administration of justice would fit the following definitions of institutional racism. James M. Jones[92] defines institutional racism as:

> **Those established laws, customs, and practices which systematically reflect and produce racial inequities in American society. If racist consequences accrue to institutional laws, customs, or practices, the institution is racist whether or not the individuals maintaining those practices have racist intentions.[93]**

He also refers to Haas's concise definition of institutional racism, which is defined as "the set of policies, practices, and procedures that adversely affect some ethnic (or racial) groups so that they will be unable to rise to a position of equality.[94] This latter definition is related to Galster and Hill's definition, which emphasizes the economic ramifications of institutional racism for racial groups vying for scarce resources within an urban milieu, and states "institutionalized racism involves less-obvious connections between flows of resources and power over metropolitan space, resulting in African- and European-Americans having different starting points in their quest for individual and group economic success."[95]

SUMMARY AND DISCUSSION

In its essence racial profiling is an old phenomenon in the United States. The disproportionate attention paid to African Americans has been occurring since at least the end of the Civil War. Wintersmith[96] discusses the history of the problematic relationship between the police and the black community, suggesting that the relationship established in the era of slavery continued after slavery into the 20th century. David Orshinsky[97] details a sordid criminal justice system: the convict lease system, which began in Mississippi in the 1860s and spread throughout the South. Under this system, police would conduct sweeps of the streets for vagrants, loiterers, and trespassers, arresting hundreds, the majority of which were black, who were leased to companies by the state for a fee as inexpensive labor. They were treated worse than slaves, with many dying before they could finish the term of their sentence because, as opposed to slaves, they had no value, and they could be easily replaced with another black prisoner.[98]

The Kerner Commission[99] also focused on the antagonistic relationship between the police and blacks as a major factor in the riots of the mid-1960s. Thus, racial profiling as discussed here can be seen as a part of the continuing problematic relationship between law enforcement and by extension the criminal justice system, and the African American community.

Two U.S. Supreme Court decisions appear to provide law enforcement with wide discretion in stopping vehicles being driven by blacks. In *Terry v. Ohio* in

1968 the Court established that the Fourth Amendment permits police to stop a person for questioning when they have a "reasonable suspicion" that criminal activity may be taking place. In *Whren v. United States* the Court increased the discretionary powers of law enforcement.[100] This, of course, means that courts give deference to police discretion, making it difficult for minority plaintiffs to win suits claiming racial discrimination in police encounters.

We use the term "spatial profiling" to characterize the practice of law enforcement when it concentrates in geographic areas distinguished by the race of the population. It can be seen as a social control mechanism used by law enforcement, intentionally or unintentionally, to surveil and circumscribe the actions and movement of specific racial/ethnic groups.

NOTES

1. Report of the National Advisory Commission on Civil Disorders (New York: Bantam Books, 1968).

2. D. Harris, *Driving While Black: Racial Profiling on Our Nation's Highways* (New York: ACLU Department of Public Education, 1999).

3. J. Feagin, *Racist America: Roots, Current Realities, and Future Reparations* (New York: Routledge, 2000).

4. Harris, *Driving While Black: Racial Profiling on Our Nation's Highways*; D. Harris, (1999). "The Stories, the Statistics, and the Law: Measuring "Driving While Black," *Minnesota Law Review 84*.

5. T. Ginsberg & H. Goldman, "Firing of N.J. Police Superintendent Adds Fuel to Racial-Profiling Debate," *Knight Ridder/Tribune News Service*, March 2, 1999; Harris, *Driving While Black: Racial Profiling on Our Nation's Highways*.

6. Ginsberg & Goldman, "Firing of N.J. Police Superintendent Adds Fuel to Racial-Profiling Debate."

7. Ibid.

8. T. Minton (2010). *Jail Inmates at Midyear 2009—Statistical Tables*. Bureau of Justice Statistics. Retrieved at http://bjs.ojp.usdoj.gov/content/pub/pdf/jim09st.pdf

9. H. West (2010). *Prison Inmates at Midyear 2009—Statistical Tables*. Bureau of Justice Statistics. Retrieved at http://bjs.ojp.usdoj.gov/index.cfm?ty=pbdetail&iid=2200

10. M. Mauer, *Racial Disparities in the Criminal Justice System: Testimony Prepared for the House Judiciary Subcommittee on Crime, Terrorism, and Homeland Security*. October 29, 2009, Washington, DC: The Sentencing Project.

11. J. Fellner (2009). "Race, Drugs, and Law Enforcement in the United States." *Stanford Law & Policy Review 20*(2): 257–291.

12. Human Rights Watch, *Incarcerated America* (April 2003). Available at http://hrw.org/backgrounder/usa/incarceration/.

13. D. Harris. *Profiles in Injustice: Why Racial Profiling Cannot Work* (New York: The New Press, 2002).

14. Feagin, *Racist America*.

15. D. Milovanovic & K. Russell, eds. *Petit Apartheid in the U.S. Criminal Justice System* (Durham, NC: Carolina Academic Press, 2001); Feagin, *Racist America*; Ibid.

16. Harris, *Driving While Black*.

17. Ibid.

18. Harris, *Profiles in Injustice*.

19. J. Lamberth. *State of New Jersey vs. Pedro Soto*, 1996, p. 66.

20. Harris, *Driving While Black*.

21. Ibid.

22. R. L. Smith & D. Davis, "Migration Patterns Hold Back Cleveland: Segregation Takes Economic Toll, Analysts Say," *The Plain Dealer*, 2002, p. 8.

23. Mayor's Investigative Report on the Presence of Racist Activity within the Cleveland Police Department.

24. S. Patton (2009). America on Lockdown: New Facts about America's Prisons & Prisoners. Legal Defense Fund. Retrieved at http://www.thedefendersonline .com/2009/02/03/america-on-lockdown-new-facts-about-america%E2%80%99s-prisons-prisoners/

25. "The Sentencing Project" (2010). *Racial Disparity*. Retrieved at http://www .sentencingproject.org/template/page.cfm?id=122

26. Patton, *America on Lockdown*.

27. D. Schrantz, *Reducing Racial Disparity in the Criminal Justice System* (Washington D.C.: The Sentencing Project, 2000).

28. E. Anderson, *Code of the Street: Decency, Violence, and the Moral Life of the Inner City* (New York: W.W. Norton, 2000).

29. W. Wilbanks, *Myth of a Racist Criminal Justice System* (Monterey, CA: Brooks/ Cole, 1987); H. MacDonald, *Are Cops Racist? How the War Against the Police Harms Black Americans* (Chicago: Ivan R. Dee, 2003).

30. Tonry, *Malign Neglect—Race, Crime, and Punishment in America* (city of publication: publisher, date).

31. B. MacLean & D. Milovanovic, eds., *Racism, Empiricism, and Criminal Justice* (Vancouver: Collective Press, 1990).

32. Wilbanks, *Myth of a Racist Criminal Justice System*; Ibid.

33. S. R. Cureton (2000). "Justifiable Arrests or Discretionary Justice: Predictors of Racial Arrest Differentials," *Journal of Black Studies* 30(5): p. 17.

34. Blumstein acknowledges the questionable use of arrest data as a valid indicator of the race of those who commit crimes, or whether arrest statistics reflect

police discrimination (intended or not) in who they arrest. To address this matter, he cites the work of Hindelang, which showed a strong correspondence between offender's race as reported by victims in the National Crime Survey and arrestee racial data for the same type of crimes. Michael Hindelang (1978). "Race and Involvement in Common Law Personal Crimes," *American Sociological Review* 43:93.

35. A. Blumstein (1993). "Racial Disproportionality of U.S. Prison Populations Revisited," *University of Colorado Law Review 64.*

36. Ibid.

37. Ibid.

38. Ibid.

39. Ibid., p. 754.

40. Tonry, *Malign Neglect—Race, Crime, and Punishment in America.*

41. Ibid., pp. 68–69.

42. Ibid.; Blumstein, "Racial Disproportionality."

43. Wilbanks, *Myth of a Racist Criminal Justice System*; MacLean & Milovanovic, eds., *Racism, Empiricism, and Criminal Justice.*

44. C. Mann, *Unequal Justice: A Question of Color.* (Bloomington, IN: Indiana University Press, 1993).

45. R. Quinney, *The Social Reality of Crime* (Boston: Little, Brown, & Co., 1970); W. S. R. Chambliss, *Law, Order, and Power* (Reading, MA: Addison-Wesley, 1971).

46. D. Hawkins (1987). "Beyond Anomalies: Rethinking the Conflict Perspective on Race and Criminal Punishment," *Social Forces*, 65: p. 27; J. C. W. Bauer, (1997). "Generating Fear: The Politics of Crime Reporting," *Crime, Law, and Social Change*, 27: p. 21; P. Gordon (1988). "Black People and the Criminal Law: Rhetoric and Reality," *International Journal of the Sociology of Law*, 16: p. 19; M. Lynch & E. Patterson, *Justice with Prejudice* (Guilderland, NY: Harrow and Heston, 1996).

47. M. DeLisi & B. Regoli (1999). Race, Conventional Crime, and Criminal Justice: The Declining Importance of Skin Color," *Journal of Criminal Justice*, 27(6): p. 9. R. Weitzer, (1996). "Racial Discrimination in the Criminal Justice System: Findings and Problems in the Literature," *Journal of Criminal Justice*, 24(4): p. 14.

48. Hawkins, "Beyond Anomalies."

49. Mann, *Unequal Justice.*

50. Cureton, "Justifiable Arrests or Discretionary Justice."

51. G. R. Bridges, Crutchfield, & E. Simpson (1987). "Crime, Social Structure, and Criminal Punishment: White and Nonwhite Rates of Imprisonment." *Social Problems*, 34(4).

52. Ibid.

53. Ibid.

54. MacLean & Milovanovic, eds., *Racism, Empiricism, and Criminal Justice*; Milovanovic and Russell, eds., *Petit Apartheid in the U.S. Criminal Justice System*.

55. MacLean & Milovanovic, eds., *Racism, Empiricism, and Criminal Justice*, pp. 12–13.

56. Blumstein, "Racial Disproportionality"; R. Kennedy, *Race, Crime, and the Law* (New York: Pantheon Books, 1997); R. Kennedy (1994). "The State, Criminal Law, and Racial Discrimination: A Comment," *Harvard Law Review*, 107.

57. Bridges, et al., "Crime, Social Structure, and Criminal Punishment"; D. Cole, (1995). "The Paradox of Race and Crime: A Comment on Randall Kennedy's 'Politics of Distinction,'" *Georgetown Law Journal, 83*.

58. Mann, *Unequal Justice*, p. 139.

59. Bridges, et al., "Crime, Social Structure, and Criminal Punishment"; Cureton, "Justifiable Arrests or Discretionary Justice"; MacLean & Milovanovic, eds., *Racism, Empiricism, and Criminal Justice*.

60. L. Wacquant, *Deadly Symbiosis: When Ghetto and Prison Meet and Merge* (Thousand Oaks, CA: Sage, 2001).

61. Feagin, *Racist America:Roots, Current Realities, and Future Reparations*.

62. R. F. Wintersmith, *The Police and the Black Community* (Lexington, MA: Lexington Books, 1974), pp. 12–13.

63. Ibid., p. 18.

64. Ibid.; Wacquant, *Deadly Symbiosis: When Ghetto and Prison Meet and Merge*.

65. Feagin, *Racist America: Roots, Current Realities, and Future Reparations*, p. 146.

66. D. S. Massey, & N. A. Denton. *American Apartheid* (Cambridge: Harvard University Press, 1993); M. L. Oliver, & T. Shapiro. *Black Wealth/White Wealth* (London: Routledge, 1997); W. D. Keating, N. Krumholz, & D. C. Perry, (eds.). *Cleveland: A Metropolitan Reader* (Kent, OH: Kent State University Press, 1995); P. Hayes (1999). *Blacklisted: An Investigation of Racial Profiling*. WKYC Television News.

67. J. M. Jones. *Prejudice and Racism* (Reading, MA: Addison-Wesley 1972).

68. K. L. Kusmer. *A Ghetto Takes Shape* (Urbana and Chicago: University of Illinois Press, 1976).

69. Wintersmith, *The Police and the Black Community*, p. 44.

70. Siegal & Senna, *Juvenile Delinquency* (St. Paul, MN: West Publishing Company, 1997).

71. P. A. Langan, L. A. Greenfeld, S. K. Smith, M. R. Durose, & D. J. Levin (2001). *Police-Public Contact Survey*. Washington, DC.; Harris, *Profiles in Injustice*.

72. Siegal & Senna, *Juvenile Delinquency*.

73. D. A. Smith & C. A. Visher (1981). "Street-level Justice: Situational Determinants of Police Arrest Decisions," *Social Problems* 29(2): p. 11.

74. Siegal & Senna, *Juvenile Delinquency*.

75. K. Turner, "A Lawman's Legacy," *The Plain Dealer Sunday Magazine*, October 26, 2003.

76. *Terry v. Ohio* Symposium Issue (1998). *St. John's Law Review*, 72: p. 826.

77. Turner, "A Lawman's Legacy."

78. *Whren v. United States*, 517 U.S. 806 (1996).

79. D. Harris (1998). "Particularized Suspicion, Categorical Judgments: Supreme Court Rhetoric versus Lower Court Reality under *Terry v. Ohio*," *St. John's Law Review* 72; p. 2.

80. Ibid., p. 2.

81. Ibid.

82. Smith (1981). Street-level justice.

83. K. C. Davis, *Police Discretion* (St. Paul, MN: West Publishing Co., 1975).

84. D. Black, *The Behavior of Law* (New York: Academic Press, 1976); W. Cook, (1967). "Policemen in Society: Which Side Are They On?" *Berkeley Journal of Sociology*, 12: p. 13; J. Galliher (1971). "Explanations of Police Behavior," *Sociological Quarterly*, 12: p. 11.

85. R. Park, *The City: Suggestions for the Investigation of Human Behaviour* (Chicago: University of Chicago Press, 1925).

86. M. Foucault, *Discipline & Punish: The Birth of the Prison* (New York: Vintage Books, 1977), p. 78.

87. Ibid., p. 272.

88. N. Websdale, *Policing the Poor* (Boston: Northeastern University Press, 2001).

89. Wacquant, *Deadly Symbiosis: When Ghetto and Prison Meet and Merge.*

90. Ibid.

91. J. Rajchman, *Foucault's Art of Seeing, in Philosophical Events: Essays of the 80s* (Columbia University Press: New York, 1991).

92. J. M. Jones, *Prejudice and Racism* (Reading, MA: Addison-Wesley Publishing Co., 1997).

93. Ibid., p. 438.

94. Ibid.

95. G. C. Galster & E. W. Hill, eds., *The Metropolis in Black & White: Place, Power, and Polarization* (Rutgers, NJ: State University of New Jersey, 1992), p. 2.

96. R. F. Wintersmith, *The Police and the Black Community* (Lexington, MA: Lexington Books, 1974).

97. D. M. Osinsky, *"Worse than Slavery": Parchman Farm and the Ordeal of Jim Crow* (New York: Free Press Paperbacks, 1996).

98. This practice was finally ended—as a formal practice (as Douglas Blackmon has shown in his book, *Another Name for Slavery* [New York: Doubleday, 2008] this practice continued illegally in another form for another decade or two)—in the

1920s, not because of the moral arguments against it. Rather, organized labor and industry opposed this cheap labor and in 1929 pressured Congress to pass the Hawes Cooper Act, along with the Ashurst-Sumners Act. See United States Prison Industries Reorganization Administration, *The Prison Labor Problem in Tennessee* (Washington, DC: Prison Industries Reorganization Administration, 1937).

99. Report of the National Advisory Commission on Civil Disorders.

100. K. S. Glover, *Racial Profiling: Research, Racism, and Resistance* (Lanham: Rowman & Littlefield, 2009).

2

RACIAL PROFILING

Although some political and social commentators have begun to suggest that America has now entered an era of post-racialism with the election of Barack Obama, its first African American president, ironically it was the arrest of President Obama's personal friend, prominent African American, Harvard scholar, Henry Louis "Skip" Gates, at his home in Cambridge, Massachusetts, by a white police officer, a mere seven months after Obama's inauguration, that would serve as the first attention-grabbing sign of the faultiness of this notion of a "post-racial America." This arrest which Gates alleged was a case of racial profiling was not only a reality check for the nation and a refutation of the premise of post-racialism, it was also a reminder for Gates and other elite or "exceptional" blacks of their continued membership among the lower racial caste within the structure of America's racially/ethnically stratified social hierarchy.[1]

Racial profiling transcends all social strata within the black community and is a common denominator in the experiences of persons of African descent in encounters with law enforcement and the police in America. Racial profiling is arguably one of the last things that all black people have in common. From the class divisions between low-income and middle-class blacks as exemplified in Bill Cosby's critique of the educational failings of lower-class blacks, the Pew Research Center's recent report on the estrangement of middle-class blacks from their lower-income brethren, and Eugene Robinson's contentions in his recent book, *Disintegration: The Splintering of Black America*, to the questioning of whether presidential candidate Barack Obama was authentically black enough by other blacks, racial profiling represents one of the last overt vestiges of racial oppression that is common to all blacks, regardless of socioeconomic status, educational level, religion or denomination, political affiliation, occupation, or residence. As Malcolm X stated in his famed "Ballot or the Bullet" speech which he gave at Cory United Methodist Church in Cleveland in 1964, "whether you're a Christian or a Muslim or a Nationalist . . . We (black people) all have the same problem. They don't hang you because you're Baptist; they hang you because you're black!" Malcolm's point is that despite what superficial social status blacks might perceive their various titles or affiliations as conferring upon them that distinguishes them from other blacks, in the eyes of the dominant culture, including law enforcement, they were all the same, "black" and are equally treated accordingly.

The Case of Robert L. Wilkins

On May 8, 1992, a Harvard Law graduate and attorney with the District of Columbia Public Defender Service was stopped by Maryland state troopers as he was driving back to Washington along with several of his relatives in a rented car from the funeral of his grandfather.[2] Although Wilkins balked at the search request citing the probable cause requirement for a search, the troopers insisted on searching the car, forcing the party out of the car as dogs sniffed, and of course, found no contraband. Standing beside the road between 6:00 and 7:00 a.m. while troopers milled about and the German shepherd sniffed the car was, of course, very embarrassing to the group.

Wilkins went to the ACLU who agreed to take the case and file a lawsuit against the Maryland state police for profiling. After filing the suit, Wilkins and the ACLU received the police intelligence report from the Maryland state police. This report advised state troopers that drug traffickers were predominately black males and females, generally traveling early in the morning or late at night, and they favored rental cars with Virginia registration. Wilkins and his relatives received a settlement in the suit, amounting to $50,000 in damages plus $46,000 in attorney's fees. The state also agreed to stop using race-based drug courier profiles as law enforcement tools, and also to train new and previously employed state police on the policy, and importantly they agreed to track the reason for traffic stops and the race of the person stopped. This information would be used by the court to monitor the conduct of the Maryland State Police.

The police reports had stated that 70 to 75 percent of people searched on I-95 were African American, even though they "represented only 17 percent of those driving on the highway and only 17 percent of traffic violators." Nevertheless the rate of finding contraband among white drivers was four times that of black drivers.

Racial Profiling Across the Race

To illustrate the nature and breadth of racial profiling, Ogletree provided 100 cases of general racial profiling against professional black men in his recent book[3]: He divided the 100 cases into several categories:

- Driving while black
- Wrongfully suspected of criminal conduct by law enforcement officials
- Wrongfully suspected of criminal conduct by members of the public
- The unwarranted fear of black men
- The assumption that all black men are or should be in service or support positions
- Unwarranted police aggravation
- Unwarranted race assumptions in academic and professional settings
- General race matters

The "driving while black" list includes stories about such prominent African Americans as Justice Thurgood Marshall, John Hope Franklin, Johnnie Cochran, Jr., Julian Bond, Roger Wilkins, and William Julius Wilson. They and the others told stories of being racially profiled. The list included judges, several Harvard, Stanford, and other law school graduates, law professors, Attorney General Eric Holder (while a college student at Columbia University), university professors, engineers, and movie stars.

Both of the coauthors of this book have had several encounters of racial profiling by police officers. One of us, Wornie Reed, has had encounters going back to the 1960s, when such police behavior was thought to occur more readily. The issue in the current context is that such behavior continues. An example of a more recent encounter is provided below by Ronnie Dunn, in his own words.

ON BEING RACIALLY PROFILED: RONNIE DUNN

On two occasions, I have found myself a subject and unwitting participant in encounters that could be used as data in research on racial profiling. The first incident occurred while conducting research for the project reported in this book. Living at the time in an inner-ring suburb just east of the city approximately 15 minutes from downtown Cleveland by freeway, I typically used the interstate to commute to the downtown campus of the urban university I attended and currently work at. However, on this particular chilly autumn day in which I had a business meeting, traffic was backed up on the freeway; therefore, I exited the interstate and took the city streets into downtown.

After exiting the freeway traveling west along St. Clair Avenue, a major east/west traffic artery, I entered the predominately black neighborhood of Glenville, the site of a race riot in 1968, which lasted five days and left seven people (one civilian, three police, and three black nationalists) dead and 15 wounded, including 11 police officers.[4] As I proceeded down this broad boulevard with two lanes of traffic in each direction, I was startled as out of my peripheral vision I observed a vehicle pulling alongside me, riding in the curb lane. I turned to see a Cleveland police officer riding in a black-and-white cruiser with his window rolled down on this nippy, 50-plus degree morning. The officer's face was beet red and wore a discernible scowl. After the officer was apparently able to get a visual of who was driving this clean, burgundy Lexus ES 300 (the car was about seven years old at the time but very well maintained), he immediately dropped back along my right-rear fender and began to run a check on my license plate.

While I knew I hadn't violated any traffic laws and was not concerned about having a police record, I was aware of and concerned about the potential for such encounters with the police to end tragically. Therefore, I reached for my cell phone and called both my coauthor (Reed whom I worked for at the time) and another friend who was a doctoral student at the time and left messages on their voicemail informing them of what was taking place. Feelings of humiliation, frustration, and anger began to wash over me as I led a procession of cars down this busy city street during the morning rush hour. The officer trailed me for at least two cityblocks. It was reminiscent of O. J. Simpson in the white Ford Bronco leading the police on the slow-speed chase down California's I-405 highway. It was obvious that no cars were going to pass me or the officer as others looked on in wonder.

My attention, however, was momentarily diverted during this surreal encounter by the reaction of a group of four or five middle-school-aged African American boys I observed walking along the sidewalk on the opposite side of the street on their way to school. I could see the look of excited curiosity on their face and read their lips, as they observed this scene and asked "Ooh, I wonder what he did?" This question and my perception of the impact this image would have on these young black boys on their way to school, troubled me. I was an ostensibly successful black man, in a suit and tie (which ironically I had worn for my meeting later that day with the executive director of a nonprofit organization that dealt with racial and social issues in the city to discuss the issue of racial profiling), driving a nice car on his way to an office building downtown, which reflects everything society tells them they should go to school to strive to achieve, being trailed by the police for no apparent reason.

Just as quickly as the police officer's car had appeared, it disappeared, having turned off on a side street after my license plate came back clean, as I knew it would. Also upsetting was the fact that I was unable to get the number of the police cruiser due to its position near my right-rear fender during the encounter. As I sat at the next red light, a young African American male pulled up next to me and motioned for me to roll down my window. He asked, "Man did you see that s*#!? That cop was running your plates!" I told him, "I know." He continued expressing his disapproval with a few more explicit statements. I then asked him if he minded giving me his name and number as a witness to what he had observed. He agreed, and I jotted down his name and number on the morning newspaper in the seat next to me. I intended to lodge a complaint against this officer.

I proceeded on to my office at the university reflecting on the chain of events and getting more and more incensed as I thought of how I had served my country, serving in the military, gone to school to get an education and better myself, only to be harassed and treated unjustly by the police for no apparent reason, other than the color of my skin. For if the officer had a valid reason for his actions or if I had violated a traffic law, I would have preferred he stop me and issue me a ticket. At least that way I would have known why I had become the object of his police action.

Once in my office, I called the Sixth District, the precinct in which the incident had occurred. I told the desk sergeant of the incident and wanted to know which officers were on patrol in that particular zone at that time of the morning. He stated that he could not determine which patrol car it might have been or who the officer might have been. Needless to say, I did not believe this to be true, but I was powerless to compel the officer to provide me with the information or to assist me in voicing my complaint.

Undeterred, I then called the office of the councilman in whose ward the incident had occurred. The councilman, an African American I knew personally, had not arrived at work yet, but his aide asked if she could help me. I described the incident to her and the outcome of my call to the police district. I also gave her a physical description of the officer and she immediately had the name of an officer she thought it could be. I was struck and dismayed that this officer's behavior was such that it had obviously already come to the attention of city hall, and yet it evidently persisted. She said she would relay the information to the councilman when he arrived and have him give me a call. I was so anxious to have the issue addressed, I called back within the hour and the councilman was in. He had been informed of the situation and acknowledged that he also suspected it was the officer his aide had identified and indicated he was known for such behavior. He suggested I call the commander at the Sixth District, whom he stated was "a brother" and "was cool." I did and once I had explained the incident to the commander, I was not too surprised when he automatically began to defend the actions of his officer. Unfortunately, I, like far too many blacks and other persons of color who have been subjected to such treatment by the police, had come to expect that our complaints to police officials would fall on deaf ears.

When I told the commander that I believed my civil rights had been violated, he asked "What civil right had been violated?" I realized at this point the difficulty of proving such a charge when a stop had not been made, and that while the officer technically might not have violated my Fourth Amendment right against "unreasonable search and seizure" and it was questionable whether he violated my 14th Amendment right of "equal protection under the law," the sense of injustice that I felt from this officer's actions was not diminished the least bit. I then said that "I had been racially profiled," to which the commander replied, "the 16- and 17-year-old teenagers, hanging out on the corner of E. 116th and St. Clair with their pants hanging around their butts claim that we racially profile them." Incredulous that he would try to invalidate the legitimacy of my complaint by comparing me to individuals whom he implied fit the "profile" of drug dealers, I retorted, "Now wait a minute! While there might be hollow claims of racial profiling, you cannot tell me that there are not legitimate claims as well." I then told him of how the group of school-aged black boys had witnessed this chain of events and the negative impact that the image of an African American male, that from all outward appearances symbolized the "role model" they are told to go to school and get an education to emulate, being harassed by the police for no obvious reason. This juxtaposed against the image of young black drug dealers the commander described being searched by the police for suspected drug activity. The boys could conclude, "Why bother trying to do the right thing and get an education and be successful if you are still going to be treated like a criminal by the police?" Why not just "avoid the rush and go the route of least resistance?"

At this point the commander's tone changed. "Well what can we [the police] do to address it [racial profiling]?" he asked. I replied, "You can begin by not denying it out-of-hand, but at least take a look at and examine such complaints." I went on to explain to him that I was conducting research on this very issue and that complaints of racial profiling need to be investigated in order to protect citizens from abuse as well as to build trust in the police within the community, and enhance police–community relations, particularly in the African American community. While the commander became less defensive and indicated that he was interested in trying to work to address the problems that contribute to the abrasive relationship between the police and the African American community, it was apparent by now that I would not receive sufficient information regarding the identity of the offending officer in order to file a formal complaint, and thus the grievance would go no further. The conversation with the commander ended amicably with us agreeing to continue to work from our respective positions to address this issue.

RACIAL PROFILING AND DRIVING WHILE BLACK

Prior to September 11th a review on the subject of racial profiling using various social science databases resulted in very little in the way of articles written in social science journals. The majority of the articles written on the subject to that point were found in legal journals while the bulk of those on the subject of "driving while black" appeared in newspapers or in what is referred to as "gray literature," popular magazines and periodicals such as *Newsweek* and *Time*. The preponderance of the evidence in these articles was anecdotal data, which is frequently dismissed within many scientific and public policy discussions as "the isolated experiences of disgruntled, angry, or hypersensitive minorities."[5] The most often cited empirical study was conducted by Temple University Professor John Lamberth. Lamberth's research has been cited in expert testimony in landmark racial profiling lawsuits brought against the New Jersey State Police and the Maryland State Police.

In the New Jersey study, Lamberth utilized a database with all traffic stops and arrests by state police, and data obtained from traffic and violator surveys he conducted to determine whether blacks were being stopped in disproportion to their numbers among the driving population along stretches of Interstate Highway 95 in New Jersey. Lamberth conducted his traffic survey by using teams posted at four designated sites along I-95 to record the number of vehicles, with the exception of large trucks, tractor trailers, buses, and government vehicles, that contained black motorists. These data were collected during 21 randomly selected two-and-one-half hours sessions, between 8 a.m. and 8 p.m. in June 1993.[6]

In the violator survey, Lamberth had the observation team supervisor travel a designated stretch of the N. J. Turnpike with the cruise control on his vehicle set at the posted 60 mph speed limit and record the number of vehicles that passed him, the number that he passed, and the number with black occupants. These data were gathered during 10 sessions over four days in July 1993.[7] Lamberth's use of a violator survey strengthened his research in that it provided a relatively precise measure of the percentage of speeders from each racial group to compare against the actual traffic ticketing data.

Lamberth found that blacks represented 13.5 percent of the driving population along this stretch of I-95, which was consistent with 1990 Census data for the 11 states from which almost 90 percent of the vehicles observed were registered.[8] While blacks represented 15 percent of those speeding, they were 46.2 percent of those stopped, constituting an absolute disparity of 32.7 percentage points (46.2–13.5 percent). Lamberth concluded that it was highly unlikely that such statistics could have occurred by chance.[9]

Lamberth's unpublished reports and the research methods he used in investigating the traffic enforcement practices of New Jersey State Police and the Maryland Highway Patrol were instrumental in formulating the empirical aspects of Harris's research on racial profiling.[10] Harris's articles on racial profiling, which resulted from his commissioned work for the Ohio legislature to study the issue in the state, were instrumental in the development of the American Civil Liberties Union's (ACLU's) national campaign against racial profiling by law enforcement.

Harris's work on racial profiling utilized both qualitative and quantitative data.[11] The work focused on the racial disparities in traffic tickets issued in four major metropolitan areas in Ohio. Harris obtained and analyzed traffic ticket data from the municipal courts in Toledo, Akron, Dayton, and Franklin County (Columbus). He used the physical descriptions included in the computerized case files maintained by the courts to determine the race of those ticketed. Harris's method is admittedly conservative, in that it only accounts for those cases in which a citation was written. It does not include those traffic stops where a warning or ticket was not issued. He also grouped all nonblack minorities into the category with whites, thereby further increasing the conservativeness of his findings on the racial disparity between the ticketing of blacks and nonblacks in these four metropolitan areas.

Harris's review of the traffic ticket data in Akron, Toledo, and Dayton for 1996, 1997, and 1998 and for 1996 and 1997 in Columbus/Franklin County (the only years the data were available) found that blacks were issued 37.6 percent,

31 percent, 50 percent, and 25.2 percent of the traffic tickets in these cities, respectively. Harris compared these ticketing percentages to the *driving age population* for blacks and nonblacks. He defined the driving age as persons between the ages of 15 and 75. He further refined the driving age population and increased the conservativeness of his findings by using data compiled by the Federal Highway Administration of the U.S. Department of Transportation's National Personal Transportation Survey, which showed that 21 percent of black households are without a motor vehicle. By further reducing the percentage of blacks in the driving population, this adjustment increased the probability of blacks being ticketed in each city. The likelihood of blacks being ticketed in comparison to nonblacks increased from 2.02 in Toledo and 2.04 in Akron to more than 2.7 times in both cities and from 1.8 times in Dayton and Columbus/Franklin County to 2.5 and 2.4 times, respectively.[12]

As a result of the research by Lamberth and Harris, the advocacy of the ACLU, and racial profiling lawsuits, many agencies began to collect systematic data on traffic stops. In 1999, two states had passed legislation that mandated officers to collect race data for all traffic stops.[13] By 2002, 18 states had passed legislation concerning racial profiling, most of which included data collection[14]; and by 2003 14 states had passed laws requiring racial profiling policies.

The findings from studies of this traffic stop data have been fairly consistent. Almost all of the studies have found some disparities in the rate of minorities, especially African Americans, who have been stopped, cited, searched, or arrested. For example, Petrocelli, Piquero, and Smith[15] in their study of data collected in Richmond, Virginia, found that African Americans were stopped at higher rates than whites, and they were also searched at higher rates. Hernandez-Murillo and Knowles[16] found similar results in Missouri, with Hispanics having higher rates of stops and searches in comparisons to whites than blacks. Blacks were stopped more and searched more in Boston.[17] Cordner, Williams, and Zuniga[18] found similar results in San Diego, as did Zingraff, Mason, Smith, Devey-Tomaskovic, Warren, McMurray, and Fenton[19] in North Carolina. Meehan and Ponder,[20] who found the same results in a "medium-sized suburban" town, also found an ecological distribution of racial profiling. Racial profiling of African Americans increased as they traveled farther from "black" communities and into whiter neighborhoods.

DISCUSSION

National attention on the issue of "driving while black" began in the mid-1990s with the attention generated by the New Jersey cases.[21] However, the phenomenon of being stopped for "driving while black" did not begin with New Jersey in the 1990s. Throughout the 20th century, black drivers regularly complained that they were harassed by police officers. It was common advice for black motorists to drive below the posted speed limit—but not too slow as to attract attention—because police officers would regularly stop blacks for traveling even one mile an hour faster than what was posted. Some black drivers took road trips at night, when it was harder for police to identify them by skin color as they drove down dark country roads.[22]

Thomas Sugrue[23] suggests that the phenomenon of being pulled over for "driving while black" indicates the connections between the history of the automobile and the history of African Americans. He notes that from the late 19th century through the civil rights revolution of the 1950s and 1960s, American blacks faced some of the harshest indignities of legal segregation on buses, streetcars, and trains. So whenever possible they took to automobiles to avoid the insults.

> **The car provided southern blacks a way to subvert Jim Crow. As Gunnar Myrdal noted in his exhaustive study of black America published in 1944, "the coming of the cheap automobile has meant for Southern Negroes, who can afford one, a partial emancipation from Jim Crowism." Blacks who could afford to travel by car did so as a way of resisting the everyday racial segregation of buses, trolleys, and trains . . . Driving gave southern blacks a degree of freedom that they did not have on public transportation or in most public places.[24]**

However, even though the automobile provided mobility, it did not eliminate the harassment or other problems of discrimination. Black motorists found it difficult to find motels, restaurants, or toilets to use. And in addition they frequently complained of being stopped by policemen for no reason. As the stories in this chapter indicate, the harassment persists.

NOTES

1. R. A. Dunn (2010). Race and the Relevance of Citizen Complainants Against the Police. *Administrative Theory & Praxis*, 32(4): p. 557.

2. C. Olgletree. *The Presumption of Guilt: The Arrest of Henry Louis Gates Jr. and Race* (New York: Palgrave MacMillan, 2010); R. L. Wilkins (March 30, 2000). Testimony of Robert L. Wilkins, concerning "The Traffic Stops Statistics Study Act of 1999," before the Committee on the Judiciary Subcommittee on the Constitution, Federalism and Property Rights, United States Senate, p. 2.

3. Olgletree, *The Presumption of Guilt.*

4. L. N. Moore. *Carl B. Stokes and the Rise of Black Political Power* (Urbana and Chicago: University of Illinois Press, 2003), p. 27.

5. Milovanovic & Russell (eds.). *Petit Apartheid in the U.S. Criminal Justice System.*

6. Lamberth, *State of New Jersey v. Pedro Soto* (1996).

7. Ibid.

8. This research was cited during Lamberth's testimony as an expert witness in the case, *N. J. v. Pedro,* 1996. The eleven states from which the driving population data were drawn were not cited in the article.

9. Lamberth, *State of New Jersey v. Pedro Soto* (1996).

10. Personal communication with Harris, 1999.

11. Harris, *Profiles in Injustice.*

12. Ibid.

13. K. J. Strom, & M. R. Durose. *Traffic Stop Data Collection Policies for State Police, 2001.* Washington, D. C.: Bureau of Justice Statistics, U. S. Department of Justice.

14. National Conference of State Legislatures (2001). *State Laws Address "Racial Profiling."* Washington, DC.

15. M. Petrocelli, A. Piquero, & M. Smith (2003). "Conflict Theory and Racial Profiling: An Empirical Analysis of Police Traffic Stop Data, *Journal of Criminal Justice, 31*(1): pp. 1–11.

16. R. Hernandez-Murillo, & J. Knowles (2004). "Racial Profiling or Racist Policing? Bounds Tests in Aggregate Data," *International Economic Review 45*(3): pp. 959–989.

17. K. Antonovics, & B. Knight (2009). "A New Look at Racial Profiling: Evidence from the Boston Police Department," *The Review of Economics and Statistics 91*(1): pp. 163–177.

18. C. Cordner, B. Williams, & M. Zuniga. *Vehicle Stop Study: Mid-year Report* (San Diego, CA.: San Diego Police Department, 2000); G. Cordner, B. Williams, & A. Velasco. *Vehicle Stops in San Diego: 2001 (Report).* San Diego, CA.: Eastern Kentucky University; Vanderbilt University; San Diego State University, 2002.

19. M. Zingraff, H. Mason, W. R. Smith, D. Devey-Tomaskovic, P. Warren, H. L. McMurray & C. R. Fenton. *Evaluating North Carolina State Highway Patrol Data: Citations, Warnings, and Searches in 1998.* Report submitted to North Carolina Department of Crime Control and Public Safety and North Carolina State Highway, 2000.

20. A. Meehan, & M. Ponder (2002). "Race and Place: The Ecology of Racial Profiling African American Motorists," *Justice Quarterly 19*(3): pp. 399–430.

21. Harris, *Profiles in Injustice.*

22. T. J. Sugrue. "Driving While Black: The Car and Race Relations in Modern America," *Automobile in American Life and Society* (Dearborn: Henry Ford Museum and University of Michigan, 2005). Available athttp://www.autolife .umd.umich.edu

23. Ibid.

24. Ibid.

A STUDY OF TRAFFIC TICKETING

To study the driving while black (DWB) phenomenon we investigated traffic ticketing in Cleveland, Ohio. Cleveland is the second largest city in the state of Ohio and it is the center of the state's largest metropolitan area. It is the county seat of Cuyahoga County in Northeast Ohio and sits on 6,165 square miles of land along Lake Erie at the mouth of the Cuyahoga River. The city's 431,363 population is 51 percent black, 41 percent white, and the remaining 8 percent of its residents belong to some other racial group. Cleveland is considered the third-most racially segregated metropolitan area in the country[1] with blacks primarily concentrated on the city's Eastside, whites concentrated on the Westside, and Hispanics concentrated on the near Westside.[2]

Sixty percent of the city's residents live in neighborhoods in which 90 percent or more of the residents are of the same race.[3]

The first set of data used in this study was a traffic ticket database that we obtained from the Cleveland Police Department. This database contained 503,556 tickets in all, including the 182,980 traffic tickets. The remaining tickets in the database, parking tickets and tickets written for various misdemeanor offenses, were not included in our analyses. The Cleveland Police Department began voluntarily collecting data on the race of motorists ticketed in 1999.[4] Along with the race of the motorists the tickets included the ticket citation number, the date and location of the traffic stop, the gender and birth date of the motorist, the year and make of the vehicle, the number of offenses the motorist was cited with (up to five violations can be noted on each ticket), the police district (or traffic unit) that issued the ticket, if the vehicle was involved in an accident, and whether an arrest was made. The race of the motorist, the location, the issuing police district, and the year are the primary variables on the traffic ticket that were used for analysis in this study.[5]

Of the 182,980 traffic tickets written in the city between April 1999 and May 2001, blacks received 105,706 (58 percent) of the traffic citations. Whites received 66,341 (36 percent) of the traffic tickets during this period while motorists of other races received 10,933 (6 percent) of the citations (see Table 3.1). In essence, blacks received a disproportionate share of the traffic tickets written citywide given the percentage of the driving population they comprise, while whites and other minorities received less than their proportional share of the traffic citations. As shown by the ratio of tickets received by each racial group in comparison to their percentage of the driving population in Table 3.1, blacks received almost one and a half times (1.45) their proportional share of traffic

TABLE 3.1   Tickets/Driving Population

| | Tickets | | Driving Population[1] | | Ratios[2] | |
					Tickets/DP	Likelihood
Total	182,890	—	3,072,880	—	—	—
Black	105,706	58%	1,242,418	40%	1.45	2.13
White	66,341	36	1,625,560	53	0.68	—
Other	10,933	6	204,903	7	0.86	1.26

[1]Driving population estimates taken from NOACA 2000 Compress Trip Distribution Model for the City of Cleveland. Racial group data imputed from 2000 U.S. Census to NOACA gravity model.
[2]The ticket/dp ratio reflects the percentage of tickets received for each group in comparison to their percentage of the driving population. The likelihood ratio represents the chances of nonwhites being ticketed in Cleveland in comparison to whites.

tickets, while whites received slightly more than two-thirds (0.68) of their share, and other minorities received less than their proportional share of tickets (0.86). When compared to whites, blacks driving in the city of Cleveland are more than twice as likely (2.13) to be ticketed as whites, while members of other racial groups are roughly one and one-fourth times (1.26) as likely to be ticketed.

TRAFFIC TICKETING PATTERNS WITHIN POLICE DISTRICTS

To assess the distribution of traffic tickets we examined the geographic distribution as well as the racial distribution. As mentioned above, there is a strong relationship between geographic location and race in Cleveland. The Cleveland Police Department's area of jurisdiction is divided into six districts (precincts).[1] The First and Second Precincts are located on the city's Westside, the Third Precinct is located downtown, and the Fourth, Fifth, and Sixth Precincts are located on the Eastside. Correspondingly, whites predominate in districts 1 and 2, and they are the majority in district 3. Blacks predominate in districts 4, 5, and 6 (see Table 3.2).

Although using residential racial demographic data alone is not a precise measure for assessing racial disparities in traffic-ticketing patterns, an analysis of residential racial demographic data from each of the city's six police districts juxtaposed with the traffic ticket distribution by race within each district shows the geographic nature of the racial disparity in ticketing. As expected, blacks received the overwhelming majority of tickets in districts Four, Five, and Six, where they were 93.2, 80.2, and 81.1 percent of the population,

TABLE 3.2   Racial Composition of Cleveland Police Districts

Police District	White	Black	Other
1	76.8%	12.2%	11.0%
2	73.4	10.8	15.8
3	48.8	43.4	7.8
4	5.3	93.2	1.6
5	14.9	80.2	4.9
6	16.8	81.1	2.0
Total	41.5%	51.0%	7.5%

Note: Figures are based on 2000 U.S. Census Data.

---

[1] The Cleveland Police Department realigned its districts in 2008, reducing the number from six to five districts.

respectively. They also received the majority of the tickets (57 percent) in district Three, where they were relatively close to one-half of the population (43.4 percent). In districts Four, Five, and Six, however, blacks were ticketed at rates roughly comparable to their proportion of the population: 90, 76, and 82 percent respectively. This is illustrated by the tickets to driving population (DP) ratios in Table 3.3, which are close to 1.0 (0.97, 0.95, and 1.01).

The number of tickets distributed to other minority drivers exceeded their percentage of the population in only one of the city's police districts, district 2. In the other districts they were ticketed substantially less than their proportions of the population.

Whites were ticketed at rates less than their proportions of the population in census tracts in which they were the majority and more than their population proportions in two of the districts in which they were not the majority, and about parity in the other district. This appears to be, to some extent, that drivers were ticketed disproportionately high if they were "out of place," that is, in areas where they were not the majority population; however, as can be seen in Table 3.3 the disproportionate rates for blacks were greater than that for whites. Likelihood ratios were computed to show the relative likelihood of being ticketed by race. In the heavily black populated police districts—Four, Five, and Six—blacks were approximately one-half (0.57), two-thirds (0.67), and one time (1.01), respectively, as likely to be ticketed as white motorists in the same areas. In the other districts, where they were not the majority population, the likelihood of blacks being ticketed ranged from approximately two-thirds more likely (1.61) to three and a third (3.33) more likely. While whites were more likely than blacks to be ticketed in predominantly black districts, their disproportionate rates were less than that of blacks in majority white districts. Other races were more likely to be ticketed in only one district, district 2. Otherwise, they were substantially less likely to be ticketed than whites.

DEFINING THE DRIVING POPULATION

Although the number of traffic tickets blacks receive in a particular geographical area may be known and appear high, this information alone is not enough to determine whether they or other racial minorities are being disproportionately ticketed by police. In order to make a compelling empirical argument about the disproportionate nature of ticketing of blacks or other minorities within a given jurisdiction it must first be determined what percentage of the *driving population* that group represents in that area at a particular time. The estimation of the driving population (dp) in a given city or jurisdiction is essential in studying racial disparities in traffic enforcement practices. The driving population provides a base of those persons eligible to be ticketed

TABLE 3.3 Racial Ticket Distribution by Police District

Police District	White				Black				Other			
			Ratios				Ratios				Ratios	
	Tickets	Population	Tickets/ DP	Likeli- hood	Tickets	Population	Tickets/ DP	Likeli- hood	Tickets	Population	Tickets/ DP	Likeli- hood
1	72%	76.8%	0.94	0.57%	20%	12.2%	1.64	1.74	8%	11.0%	0.73	0.78
2	55	73.4	0.75	0.30	27	10.8	2.50	3.33	18	15.8	1.14	1.52
3	40	48.8	0.82	0.62	57	43.4	1.32	1.61	3	7.8	0.38	0.46
4	9	5.3	1.70	1.75	90	93.2	0.97	0.57	1	1.6	0.63	0.37
5	21	14.9	1.41	1.48	76	80.2	0.95	0.67	3	4.9	0.61	0.43
6	17	16.8	1.01	1.00	82	81.1	1.01	1.00	1	2.0	0.50	0.50

Note: Likelihood ratios for Black and Other were computed by dividing the Black (and Other) Tickets/DP ratios by the white Tickets/DP. The White Likelihood ratios were computed by dividing the white tickets/DP by the Black tickets/DP ratios.

to compare against the number of observed traffic tickets given to members of a particular racial group in the specified geographical area.

Early studies on racial profiling used residential racial demographic data from the Census as a benchmark to juxtapose against racial traffic-ticketing data (Harris, 1999; Cordner, Williams, and Zuniga, 2000; Farrell, McDevitt, Cronin, & Pierce, 2003). Researchers have differed in their use of residential demographic data in defining and estimating the driving population. In his study of racial profiling in four of the largest cities in Ohio (Columbus, Dayton, Toledo, and Akron), David Harris used age-adjusted residential demographic data from the 2000 Census to define the driving population for each city. Harris used racial demographic data for black and nonblack residents of driving age, between the ages of 15 and 75, to define the driving population. These ages represent the lower and upper limits of persons legally driving on the roads with 15 being the youngest age at which a person can drive with a driver's permit in most states and 75 being the age at which a significant decline of a person's driving is noted.[2] Comparing the driving age population of blacks and nonblacks in each city, Harris found that blacks were more than twice as likely to be ticketed by police in each city as their nonblack counterparts. Blacks were 2.02 more likely to be ticketed than nonblacks in Toledo, 2.04 times more likely in Akron, and 1.8 times in Dayton and Columbus/Franklin County. After accounting for the reported 21 percent of black households that did not own a motor vehicle in 2000 according to the U.S. Federal Highway Administration National Personal Transportation Survey, the likelihood of blacks being ticketed in comparison to nonblacks increased to more than 2.7 times in both Toledo and Akron and to 2.5 and 2.4 times, respectively in Dayton and Columbus (Harris, 2002).

While Harris's method of benchmarking analyzes traffic-ticketing distribution patterns at the city level and provides a relatively concise estimate of city residents of driving age eligible to be ticketed, this model does not provide a precise estimate of the overall driving population in that it fails to account for the nonresident or transient motorists using city streets. There are also other limitations in the use of residential Census data in estimating the driving population in a given geographic area. First, as with Harris's study, residential Census data does not account for the racial demographic data of the nonresident motorist population. Secondly, many studies that utilize residential demographic data do not incorporate adjustments, such as Harris, for driving age and the segment of the population that do not own or have access to motor vehicles. In addition, there are critics who argue that the national Census undercounts a significant portion of the minority and homeless populations in many areas

---

[2]Fridell et al. (2004) suggests that 85 years of age is the age at which a significant decline of persons driving is observed.

(Ramirez, McDevitt, & Farrell, 2000) and while the reliability of Census data as a benchmark in examining racial profiling is debatable, as Smith and Petrocelli (2001) conclude, it will continue to be used by researchers and law enforcement agencies to examine racial profiling given its cost-efficiency and accessibility.

As stated by Farrell et al.,[6] the use of racial demographic data taken from residential population data in this manner does not provide a precise measure of the driving population in that it fails to account for those drivers on the roads who live outside the geographical area in question. Considerable portions of the traffic on a city's streets are motorists drawn from its hinterlands by various push and pull factors such as work, shopping, entertainment, and other inducements. Whereas these push and pull factors may have a differential impact on the driving habits of members of particular racial groups, for example, the unemployment rate among blacks (which is typically roughly double that of whites) in a particular region might reduce or increase their propensity to drive to a nearby city for work. As Farrell, et al., indicate, there are very limited verifiable existing data on racial differences in driving behavior on which to base such calculations. Therefore, for the purposes of this study we assumed that the driving behaviors of the different racial groups that constitute the city's driving population are equally influenced by the same push/pull factors such as work, shopping, and entertainment.

Other researchers have used Department of Motor Vehicle (DMV) data on licensed drivers living in a particular geographical area to define the driving population. Although this method might provide a picture of persons licensed to drive on the roads within a given jurisdiction, once again it does not capture the transient motorist population living outside of the designated geographical area, nor does it necessarily provide the needed racial demographic data as some states such as Ohio do not include the race of motorists on drivers licenses—only their eye and hair color, height, and weight.

Given the porous nature of a city's boundaries and roadways, the use of a gravity model as used by Farrell et al.[7] to study racial profiling in the state of Rhode Island provides a more precise method of estimating driving populations than Harris's use of the driving age population or DMV records to determine who is on a city's roadways at a given point in time.[8] As noted by Farrell et al., a considerable portion of the traffic on a city's streets are motorists drawn from surrounding cities by various push and pull factors including work, shopping, entertainment, and other inducements. Farrell et al. developed a "driving population estimate" or DPE to account for the factors that push motorists from an outside jurisdiction to the target city. This DPE included data on the portion of residents in the outlying jurisdiction that owned motor vehicles, the amount of travel time (minutes) it took to drive from the contributing jurisdiction to the target city, and the percentage of residents that drove 10 miles or more to work.[9]

Gravity models are used by professional planners such as transportation planners to provide information on the amount of interaction between areas based on the size or attraction of the areas, the characteristics of the populations living in them, and decisions the population makes particularly as it relates to travel and commerce between areas.[10] The concept of gravity models is based on Newton's Law of Universal Gravitation from the field of physics, which states "two bodies in the universe attract each other in proportion to the product of their masses, and inversely to the square of their distance apart." In their use in transportation planning, gravity models are based on the notion that the degree of interaction between any two areas is directly related to the size (attraction) of the areas, and inversely related to their distance raised to some exponent. Transportation planners use gravity models to determine the travel demands of regional populations and forecast current and future infrastructure needs such as roads, bridges, and transit system.

The Gravity Model

The gravity model used in this study to define Cleveland's driving population covers the Northeast Ohio Areawide Coordinating Agency's (NOACA) service area, which includes Cuyahoga County and the surrounding counties: Lorain, Medina, Geauga, and Lake counties. The city of Cleveland is identified separately from the remainder of Cuyahoga County in the model. According to the agency's chief technical advisor, the areas outside of the agency's service area included in the model that contribute to Cleveland's driving population are Erie, Huron, Ashland, Wayne, Summit, Portage, Trumball, Ashtabula counties, and areas of the contiguous United States beyond these abutting counties.[11]

The gravity model is presented in a matrix with the districts or counties included in the model listed as both row and column heads (see Table 3.4). For the purposes of this study only the trips under the first row and column, reflecting all trips to Cleveland from the contributing counties and from Cleveland to these counties, are of interest. Reading from left to right, the rows represent the number of trips made from Cleveland to the surrounding counties. The columns list the number of trips made from the respective counties to Cleveland. The city of Cleveland appears as both a row and column head at the vertex of the matrix, and the number of trips at this row/column intersection is counted twice in the model, reflecting internal trips made from one location to another within the city.

The racial composition of Metropolitan Cleveland's 3,072,880 driving population was defined by integrating data from the gravity model with age and racial demographic data extrapolated from the 2000 Census for the 13 counties included in the model. Although defining the driving population of a city

TABLE 3.4 2000 Compress Trip Distribution Model for All Trips to City of Cleveland in 24-Hours

Districts	City of Cleveland	Cuyahoga County-Cleveland	Lorain County	Medina	Geauga	Lake	Outside NOACA	Total
City of Cleveland	960,979	448,704	24,366	10,494	8,373	32,085	40,935	1,525,936
Cuyahoga County-Cleveland	448,747	1,517,683	60,871	26,242	30,672	59,806	93,208	2,237,229
Lorain County	24,382	60,900	577,197	14,709	729	1,411	34,235	713,563
Medina	10,531	26,216	14,715	236,726	491	1,055	61,889	351,623
Geauga	8,358	30,068	738	490	129,654	20,168	15,583	205,664
Lake	32,068	59,809	1,413	1,054	20,180	472,554	14,991	602,069
Outside NOACA	61,879	160,067	45,673	56,051	23,444	25,963	101,757	474,834
Total	1,546,944	2,304,052	724,973	345,766	213,543	613,042	362,598	6,110,918

The column and row for the City of Cleveland present the data relevant to the driving population for the City of Cleveland. Reading from left to right, the rows represent the point of origin of each trip and the columns represent the destination point of each trip. The data at the intersection of the column and row heading for the City of Cleveland (960,979) are counted twice representing trips originating and terminating within the city. Thus, Cleveland's driving population equals 3,072,930 (1,546,944 + 1,525,936) vehicle trips (motorist).

with Harris's method of using the age and racial demographic data of only the residents living within the target city does not provide an exact measure of all of the drivers on the city's roadways, this method was used in conjunction with the racial demographic census data from each contributing jurisdiction in the gravity model to further specify the driving population estimate of the target city of Cleveland. Using the same age group parameters as Harris we combined the driving age population with data from the 2000 Census detailed tables *"Sex by Age."* These data tables were downloaded from the Census Bureau website for the total population and persons of both sexes within the following racial groups from the contributing counties: White alone, Black alone, American Indian and Alaska Native alone, Asian alone, Native Hawaiian and Other Pacific Islander alone, Some other race alone, and Two or more races. All racial groups except white and black were categorized as "other."

The age cohort columns for people between the ages of 15 and 75 were compiled and totals for each racial group were computed. The total for all persons of driving age within each racial group was divided into the total driving age population for each county. The racial breakdown percentages of the driving-age population were attributed to the proportion of motorists added to Cleveland's driving population from each contributing county in the gravity model. The county totals for each racial group were then added to provide an overall total for each racial group in the 13-county region. This measurement provides a refined estimate of who is driving on the city's streets, including the race of the majority of motorists of legal driving age that live within and outside the city.

The data in the traffic ticket database was used in conjunction with the driving population derived from the gravity model and census demographic data to analyze the citywide traffic-ticketing patterns by race. First, frequencies were generated from the traffic ticket data to determine the overall percentage of blacks, whites, and motorists of other races ticketed in the city during the two-year observation period (April 1999–May 2001). The difference between the percentage of the driving population that each racial group represented and the percentage of tickets members of each group received were calculated to determine the absolute disparity between the two figures. These percentages were then used to compute a ratio reflecting the percentage of tickets received by each group in relation to their percentage of the driving population.[12] This traffic ticket-to-driving population ratio was used to compute a ratio of the likelihood of being ticketed by the police in Cleveland if a motorist is black or a member of another racial minority group in comparison to whites. A ratio of one reflects the expected proportional share of tickets for each racial group in relation to the share of the driving population that group represents.[13]

COMMUNITY SETTING AND SELECTED ARTERIAL ROUTES

We also focused on two main traffic arteries—Kinsman Road, a main traffic artery utilized primarily by black motorists, and Chester Avenue, which serves as a traffic corridor from the city's eastern suburbs to the Cleveland business district. While Chester and Kinsman are both used by motorists of all races, the former more so than the latter, the majority of motorists on Chester during rush hours are white. Both Kinsman and Chester adjoin thoroughfares that extend from more affluent eastern suburbs and transverse the predominately black, low-income and working-class inner-city communities of the Kinsman and Mt. Pleasant neighborhoods (Kinsman Road), and Hough and Fairfax (Chester Avenue).

The four communities have varied socioeconomic demographics. Mt. Pleasant, the eastern-most of the four communities, abuts the well-to-do suburb of Shaker Heights. Chagrin Boulevard, which runs east to west from Interstate Highway 271 through Shaker turns into Kinsman Road at E. 156th Street on the Cleveland border. Kinsman's 4.51-mile length runs through Mt. Pleasant with its seemingly stable commercial establishments and well-maintained working-class homes, past a city park where the city's largest annual African American community celebrations are held, to the Kinsman neighborhood, where dilapidated low-income housing and a large public housing estate sit just beyond an area of abandoned industrial sites. Mt. Pleasant is a 98.5 percent black neighborhood where 25 percent of the residents live below the poverty level. The Kinsman neighborhood is 97 percent black and 3 percent white, and has a 57 percent poverty rate. Eighty-seven percent of the single-family homes in Mt. Pleasant range in value from $40,000 to $75,000 while 98 percent of the single-family homes in the Kinsman neighborhood are below $30,000 in value.[14]

The Fourth District Police Precinct, which is located on Kinsman Road, has the largest jurisdiction among the city's six police precincts. The Mt. Pleasant and Kinsman neighborhoods collectively accounted for 11 percent (3,129) of the 28,444 drug arrests and 8 percent (424) of the 5,535 arrests for violent crimes in the city between 1999 and 2001.[15] Kinsman Road, which ends at E. 55th and Woodland Avenue, serves as one of the primary east/west arterial routes for motorists traveling to downtown Cleveland from areas on the city's predominately black southeast side. According to the city's Department of Traffic Engineering's most recent traffic volume records[16] for Kinsman Road (October 23, 1993) the daily average volume of motor vehicles along Kinsman is 52,875.

Chester Avenue is a six-lane, 3.8-mile boulevard, divided by a grass median in some areas, which separates the Hough and Fairfax neighborhoods. In 1966 black rage boiled over in Hough, which as a result of racial segregation and urban renewal had been transformed from a predominantly white middle-class neighborhood prior to WWII to a black ghetto by the early 1960s. This violent social upheaval resulted in the National Guard being called in, the death of four black residents, and millions of dollars in property damage.[17] Today, Hough is undergoing a revitalization process that has witnessed a substantial increase in the housing stock as homes ranging from the mid-$100,000s to $750,000 are replacing the glass-strewn vacant lots, and burned-out, abandoned buildings that once dotted much of this inner-city neighborhood. Many of these new spacious suburban-style homes are built on side streets that run perpendicular to the north side of Chester Avenue. While Hough is attracting middle-class residents back to this inner-city community, they are primarily black professionals as its population is 97 percent black, 2.5 percent white, and less than 1 percent of other races. In spite of the influx of middle-class residents the community still has a 41 percent poverty rate and 78 percent of the single-family housing units are still valued under $30,000.

The Fairfax community, which lies to the south of Chester, is also undergoing considerable change as it is home to the Cleveland Clinic, the city's largest employer. The majority of these new development centers around the Clinic's main campus, of which Chester is the northern boundary. New residential development has been built on the south side of Chester Avenue near a commercial shopping plaza that opened in the community in the early 1990s as part of the city's federally funded Empowerment Zone Program. While these homes are also marketed toward middle-class professionals, the majority of the neighborhood's residents are low-income and working class as 33 percent of the residents live in poverty and 98 percent of the single-family housing stock is valued under $30,000. The racial demographics of Fairfax are comparable to those in Hough with 96.5 percent blacks, 2.6 percent whites, and the remainder being of some other race.

Six percent (1,686) of Cleveland's drug arrests and 7 percent (378) of the city's violent crime arrests between 1999 and 2001 were in the Hough and Fairfax neighborhoods. The Fifth District Police Precinct, which is located on Chester Avenue at E. 106th, serves these neighborhoods and its jurisdiction extends to E. 55th Street. The lower portion of Chester Avenue, which extends west from E. 55th to E. 9th Street in Downtown Cleveland, lies within the Third Precinct's jurisdiction. The most recent traffic volume records for Chester (September 24, 2000) place the daily average traffic volume at 57,929 motor vehicles.

TRAFFIC TICKET DATA ANALYZED BY RACE AND STREET

There is a vast disparity between the number of tickets written on Chester and Kinsman over the course of the two-year study period. A total of 1,682 traffic tickets were written on Chester Avenue in comparison to the 6,366 tickets distributed on Kinsman Road. For every ticket written on Chester 3.78 tickets were given out on Kinsman, in spite of the fact that roughly 5,054 more motorists (57,929–52,875) use Chester daily than use Kinsman.

Blacks were the recipients of 61 percent (1,024) of the traffic tickets written on Chester while whites received 34 percent (579) and motorists of other races accounted for 5 percent (79) of the traffic citations. Meanwhile, on Kinsman blacks received 90 percent (5,720) of the traffic tickets compared to 9 percent (553) received by whites and 1 percent (93) going to persons of other races (see Table 3.5).

There were 91 citations written on Chester between May 1 and December 31, 1999, 66 percent (60) went to blacks, 31 percent (28) to whites, and 3 percent to persons of other races. Blacks received 94 percent (455) of the 485 tickets disseminated on Kinsman during this period while whites received 5 percent (24), and motorists of other races accounted for 1 percent (six) of the tickets.

In 2000, 1,270 traffic citations were written on Chester compared to 4,004 on Kinsman. Blacks were the recipients of 61 percent (770) of the tickets doled out on Chester compared to 34 percent (434) to whites, and 5 percent (66) to other minorities. On Kinsman blacks were 94 percent of those cited (3,766) while whites were 5 percent of those ticketed (198), and other racial group members were 1 percent of those cited (40).

During the period from January through April 2001, 321 traffic tickets were meted out along Chester Avenue, 60 percent (194) of which went to blacks, while whites were on the receiving end of 37 percent (117) of the tickets, and other minority motorists garnered 3 percent (10) of the traffic violations. Meanwhile on Kinsman 1,877 traffic tickets were dispersed during the same period, 80 percent (1,499) of which were given to black motorists, whites received 18 percent (331), and persons of other races received 2 percent of the citations (47).

While there is nothing readily evident in the traffic ticket data to explain the fluctuation in ticket distribution between 1999 and 2000, former Mayor Michael White's investigation of the Cleveland police department for alleged organized racist activity was initiated in the summer of 1999 and in protest to the investigation city police officers began a six-week work slowdown that

TABLE 3.5 Traffic Ticket/Traffic Census Data by Race and Street

Traffic Artery	Race	Total		1999 (May–Dec.)		2000 (Jan.–Dec.)		2001 (Jan.–April)	
		Tickets Received	Percentage of Tickets	Tickets Received	Percentage of Tickets	Tickets Received	Percentage of Tickets	Tickets Received	Percentage of Tickets
Chester	Black	1,024	61%	60	66%	770	61%	194	60%
	White	579	34	28	31	434	34	117	37
	Other	79	5	3	3	66	5	10	3
	Total	1,682	100	91	100	1,270	100	321	100
Kinsman	Black	5,720	90	455	94	3,766	94	1,499	80
	White	553	9	24	5	198	5	331	18
	Other	93	1	6	1	40	1	47	2
	Total	6,366	100	485	100	4,004	100	1,877	100

reportedly resulted in a 30 percent decrease in the number of tickets written citywide and decreases as high as 75 percent in some neighborhoods.[18] There also is no obvious explanation for the fluctuations in the monthly average number of tickets distributed on Chester and Kinsman in 2000 and January through April of 2001. An average of 105 tickets per month was written on Chester in 2000 compared to 80 per month during the first four months of 2001. This represents a 24 percent decrease in the monthly average of tickets distributed on Chester. During the same period a 40 percent increase was noted on Kinsman as the 2000 monthly average of 334 tickets rose to 469 per month from January through April 2001.

As reflected in Table 3.5, fluctuations were also noted in the proportion of tickets distributed to members of each racial group from year to year. There was a 5 percentage point decrease in the tickets blacks received on Chester between 1999 and 2000 followed by a 1 percentage point decrease in 2001. Meanwhile, there was a 3 percentage point increase each year in the tickets whites received on Chester as the proportion of tickets motorists of other races received on the street increased by 2 percentage points between 1999 and 2000, and decreased by 2 percentage points the following year.

A dramatic decrease in the percentage of tickets blacks received on Kinsman occurred in 2001 as the proportion dropped 14 percentage points to 80 percent after remaining constant at 94 percent in 1999 and 2000. There was a corresponding sharp increase in the percentage of tickets received by whites on Kinsman in the same years as the percentage of tickets whites received remained stable at 5 percent in 1999 and 2000 then jumped 13 percentage points to 18 percent in 2001. The proportion of tickets going to members of other races on Kinsman increased by 1 percentage point in 2001 after holding at 1 percent in 1999 and 2000. The increases in tickets received by whites and other minorities in 2001 accounted for the total 14 percent shift in ticket distribution that took place among the races between 2000 and 2001. While blacks still received a disproportionate share of the tickets written on Chester and received the bulk of the tickets on Kinsman the year-to-year analysis shows a decline in the percentage of tickets blacks received on both thoroughfares over the two-year study period. This is coupled with an increase in the percentage of tickets disseminated to whites on both traffic arteries. There is no discernible trend in the ticketing pattern of other minority motorists.

SUMMARY AND DISCUSSION

Blacks clearly received a disproportionate share of tickets. They received almost 50 percent more of the traffic tickets than whites, although they were a smaller proportion of the driving population than whites. Other nonwhites received a slightly smaller percentage of the tickets than their proportion of the driving population. Interestingly, blacks were ticketed at rates comparable to their proportions of the driving populations in the heavily black police districts of the city. On the other hand, they were up to 3.3 times more likely to be ticketed in police districts where they were only a small part of the population. This relationship manifested itself in the analysis of the ticketing on our two selected thoroughfares. Blacks received 90 percent of the tickets on Kinsman Road, the thoroughfare used heavily by blacks; and they were nearly two-thirds of the motorists ticketed on Chester Avenue, the corridor primarily used by white/suburbanites commuting from the eastern suburbs to the downtown area. This suggests spatial profiling—employing different law-enforcement practices by geographic areas that are distinguished by the racial makeup of the areas or the driving population occupying the area as illustrated by Chester; a thoroughfare primarily used by whites commuting through a black area.

Although we have demonstrated that blacks receive traffic tickets substantially beyond their proportion of the driving population, this is not conclusive proof that this ticketing is racially discriminatory. For that we will need to employ additional methods, which we will do in Chapter 5.

NOTES

1. J. Ireland & D. H. Weinberg with Erika Steinmetz. *Racial and Ethnic Residential Segregation in the United States: 1980–2000* (Washington, DC: U.S. Government Printing Office, 2002).

2. M. Salling. *Cleveland Neighborhood Conditions and Trends* (Cleveland: Maxine Goodman-Levin College of Urban Affairs, 2001).

3. R. L. Smith, & D. Davis (2002). "Migration Patterns Hold Back Cleveland: Segregation Takes Economic Toll, Analysts Say," in *The Plain Dealer*, p. 8.

4. Information obtained through personal conversation with CPD database administrator.

5. The racial data by police district are from the Mayor's Investigation on Racism within the Cleveland Police Department (2000). Driving age population data corresponding with the boundaries of the police districts were not readily available.

6. A. Farrell, J. McDevitt, S. Cronin, & E. Pierce (2003). Rhode Island Traffic Stop Statistics Act Final Report. Boston, Northeastern University, Institute of Race and Justice.

7. Ibid.

8. Ibid.

9. This data was taken from the Census journey-to-work dataset.

10. Beimborn, E., & Kennedy, R. Inside the Blackbox: Making Transportation Models Work For Livable Communities. Madison, Wis.: University of Wisconsin-Milwaukee.

11. NOACA chief technical advisor, David E. Owens suggested that the drivers contributing to the gravity model from the contiguous U.S. was negligible and therefore could be disregarded in estimating the racial composition of Cleveland's driving population (personal conversation).

12. The percentage of tickets received by each group was divided by the percentage of the driving population they represent.

13. D. Harris (2002). *Profiles in Injustice: Why Racial Profiling Cannot Work* (New York, The New Press, 2002).

14. Cuyahoga County Auditor, tax billing file, tax year 2001.

15. Center on Urban Poverty and Social Change, CAN DO DATABASE, MSASS, Case Western Reserve University.

16. Traffic volume data provided by the City of Cleveland's Department of Traffic Engineering were taken from actual counts conducted by the Cuyahoga County Engineer's Office.

17. W. D. Keating, N. Krumholz, & D. C. Perry (eds.). *Cleveland: A Metropolitan Reader* (Kent, OH, Kent State University Press, 1995), p. 23.

18. K. Scholz (1999). "Chief Warns Police: Issue Tickets or Else," *The Plain Dealer*, p. 21.

4

RACIAL PROFILING ACROSS THE STATES: LEGISLATION, PRACTICES, AND RESULTS

RACIAL PROFILING LEGISLATION

Despite clear evidence that racial profiling continues to be a problem for federal, state, and local law enforcement agencies, Congress is still failing to enact legislation to conduct comprehensive studies of the issue, studies that can inform racial profiling remedies. On the other hand, minor progress has occurred in some individual states, as half of the states have enacted legislation that addresses racial profiling.[1] See Table 4.1 below. The symbolic meaning of this legislation may be more important than its effects, as the typical provisions in the legislation consists of calls for law enforcement and other

TABLE 4.1 Racial Profiling Legislation

State/Territory	Racial Profiling Legislation	Demographic Data Collection Mandated	Description
Alabama	No	No	Officers must record race data about motorists who are issued citations, arrested, searched, or if officer uses force.
Alaska	No	No	
Arizona	No	No	Legislation in 2002 and 2003 repealed previous legislation that made racial profiling a crime; new controversial law arguably encourages racial profiling; data collection is voluntary
Arkansas	Yes	No	Calls for agencies to establish policies prohibiting or combatting racial profiling
			Written prohibitions against racial profiling
California	No	No	Written prohibitions against racial profiling
			Law mandates sensitivity training
Colorado	Yes	Yes	Calls for agencies to establish policies prohibiting or combating racial profiling
			Mandates sensitivity training
Connecticut	Yes	Yes	Calls for agencies to establish policies prohibiting or combating racial profiling
			Written prohibitions against racial profiling
			Establishes complaint procedures
DC	No	No	
Delaware	No	No	

State			
Florida	Yes	Yes	Calls for agencies to establish policies prohibiting or combating racial profiling
Georgia	No	No	
Hawaii	No	No	
Idaho	No	No	
Iowa	No	No	Data collection is voluntary
Illinois	Yes	Yes	Calls for agencies to establish policies prohibiting or combating racial profiling
Indiana	No	No	
Kansas	Yes	Yes	Calls for agencies to establish policies prohibiting or combating racial profiling Written prohibitions against racial profiling
Kentucky	Yes	Yes	Calls for agencies to establish policies prohibiting or combating racial profiling Written prohibitions against racial profiling
Louisiana	Yes	Yes	Data collection mandatory in jurisdictions that have not banned racial profiling.
Maine	No	No	
Maryland	Yes	Yes	Calls for agencies to establish policies prohibiting or combating racial profiling
Massachusetts	Yes	Yes	Calls for agencies to establish policies prohibiting or combating racial profiling
Minnesota	Yes	No	Calls for agencies to establish policies prohibiting or combating racial profiling Voluntary data collection
Michigan	No	No	
Mississippi	No	No	

(continued)

TABLE 4.1 *(Continued)*

State/Territory	Racial Profiling Legislation	Demographic Data Collection Mandated	Description
Missouri	Yes	Yes	Calls for agencies to establish policies prohibiting or combating racial profiling
Montana	Yes	No	Calls for agencies to establish policies prohibiting or combating racial profiling
Nebraska	Yes	Yes	Calls for agencies to establish policies prohibiting or combating racial profiling
			Written prohibitions against racial profiling
New Hampshire	No	No	
New Jersey	Yes	No	
New Mexico	No		Calls for agencies to establish policies prohibiting or combating racial profiling
			Written prohibitions against racial profiling
New York	No	No	
Nevada	Yes	No	Written prohibitions against racial profiling
			Several jurisdictions required to collect data.
N. Carolina	No	No	
N. Dakota	No	No	
Ohio	No	No	
Oklahoma	Yes	Yes	Calls for agencies to establish policies prohibiting or combating racial profiling
			Written prohibitions against racial profiling
Oregon	No	No	Some jurisdictions required to collect data.

Rhode Island	Yes	Yes	Calls for agencies to establish policies prohibiting or combating racial profiling
			Written prohibitions against racial profiling
S. Carolina	No	No	
S. Dakota	No	No	
Tennessee	Yes	Yes	Calls for agencies to establish policies prohibiting or combating racial profiling
Texas	Yes	Yes	Calls for agencies to establish policies prohibiting or combating racial profiling
			Written prohibitions against racial profiling
Utah	Yes	Yes	Calls for agencies to establish policies prohibiting or combatting racial profiling
Vermont	No	No	
Virginia	No	No	A bill was enacted in April, 2002, to ensure cultural sensitivity by all police officers. Some jurisdictions required to collect data
Washington	Yes	Yes	Calls for agencies to establish policies prohibiting or combating racial profiling
W. Virginia	Yes	No	Calls for agencies to establish policies prohibiting or combating racial profiling
			Written prohibitions against racial profiling
Wisconsin	Yes	No	
Wyoming	Yes	No	Data collection is voluntary

Note: Information in table was collected from multiple sources, which may have been prepared at different times, meaning the snapshot suggested in the table may not be reflective of a specific time in the recent past.

Sources: ACLU and Rights Working Group. 2009. *The Persistence of Racial and Ethnic Profiling in the United States 40*; Racial Profiling Data Collection Center at Northeastern University. *Legislation and Litigation.* Retrieved from http://www.racialprofilinganalysis.neu.edu.

state agencies to establish policies prohibiting or combating racial profiling. This is, of course, a very weak response to the very real problem of racial profiling. Twelve of these states have included written prohibitions of racial profiling into their state codes, even though the practice is already forbidden by the U.S. Constitution.[2] At least these states have made initial steps toward addressing the issue. In effect, this is an admission of the existence of the racial profiling.

A comprehensive approach for addressing and eliminating racial profiling is thought to include at least three things: (1) a ban on the practice of racial profiling, (2) ample data collection, and (3) a mechanism for creating and implementing strategies to address racial profiling when it is detected.[3] Some of the states (fewer than 25 percent) have symbolic approaches to step 1, banning racial profiling. A similar proportion mandates the collection of data in traffic stops to assess racial profiling, but few have established mechanisms for creating strategies to address racial profiling when it is found in the data.

TRAFFIC STOPS, SEARCHES, AND YIELDS

In the late 1990s, as a result of widespread allegations of racial profiling (e.g., "driving while black") jurisdictions around the country began to track information about those who are stopped, searched, ticketed, and/or arrested by police officers. We reviewed some of this data from the websites of several individual states. A basic pattern emerged in the analysis of data from 13 states: blacks and Hispanics were *stopped* at greater rates than white drivers, and they were *searched* at greater rates than white drivers. We obtained data on the percent of traffic stops by race for 12 states. For Tennessee, traffic stop data were expressed as a percent of all drivers stopped for each race/ethnicity. See Table 4.2. In 11 of these 12 states blacks were stopped at higher rates than would be expected if there is equity in the rate of being stopped. For example, in Illinois, blacks were 13 percent of the drivers in the state; however, they were 18 percent of the drivers that were stopped, a rate over one-third (18/13) higher than equity. For the other 10 states the stop rates were compared to the population percentages.

Data for Hispanics were available for 11 of the states, showing excess rates of stopping Hispanic drivers in five states. In two states, Nebraska and Texas, Hispanics were stopped at rates that were less than their proportion of the population.

Data were obtained on the search rates by race for 12 states. Vehicles driven by black drivers were searched at higher rates than whites in nine of these states. Two states, Connecticut and North Carolina, reported the data as a percent of all drivers searched, while the others provided data on the rates of searches of stopped vehicles by race. In Connecticut, blacks were 23 percent of the drivers of all vehicles that were searched, nearly three times their proportion of the state population. In North Carolina nearly one-half (46 percent) of all vehicles searched had black drivers, a rate more than twice their proportion of the population. The disproportionality was even greater for Hispanics. In 9 of 10 states Hispanics were searched at higher rates than whites.

The critical issue is the yield, or hit rate, for the searches of vehicles. In other words, is there a criminal justice reason for the stopping and searching of vehicles driven by black and Hispanic drivers at disproportionately high rates in comparison to their proportions in the population, or to their proportion of cars stopped? Do blacks and Hispanics tend to have contraband in their vehicles at higher rates than whites? For the states shown in Table 4.2 the answer is clearly no. Of the nine states providing yield data, blacks had lower yields than whites in six cases, and Hispanics had lower yields than whites in seven of eight cases. In addition, there were two states, Illinois and Rhode Island, that did not provide yield data for blacks and Hispanics specifically, but provided data for "minorities." In both of these states, minorities had lower yields than whites. In 11 states with yield data, whites were guilty of carrying contraband more often than blacks or minorities in eight states, and more often than Hispanics or minorities in nine states. Thus, this apparent profiling of blacks and Hispanics were inappropriate.

SUMMARY AND DISCUSSION

Thirteen states collect data on traffic stops, including race and rates of searches as well as yield rates. We have analyzed this data to demonstrate racial biases in the law enforcement practices in several of the states. In comparison to their proportions of the population, black and Hispanic motorists are stopped excessively. Both blacks and Hispanics are searched at disproportionately high rates. These activities by law enforcement must qualify as racial profiling, as there is not criminal justice reason for the higher rates of searches in comparison to whites. This is demonstrated by the fact that the yield rate from the searches tend to be lower for blacks and Hispanics than for whites. Consequently this activity is both unfair and inefficient.

TABLE 4.2 Traffic Stops, Searches, and Yields for Selected States, by race

State	Percent of Population			Percent of All Traffic Stops		
	White	Black	Hispanic	White	Black	Hispanic
Arizona (2009)	78	4	1	62	5	25
Connecticut (2001)	87	8		84	12	
Illinois (2009)	76	13[a]	11[a]	68	18	11
Iowa (2003)	95	2	2	88	3	3
Kentucky (2001)	90	7	1	90	8	2
Minnesota (2003)	87	4	3	75	14	6
Missouri (2008)	84	11	2	79	17	2
Nebraska (2009)	84	5	8	85	6	7
N. Carolina (1997)	73	22	2	72	22	5
Rhode Island (2004–2005)	85	5	9	81	8	9
Tennessee (2006)	79	16	4	5[c]	5[c]	9[c]
Texas (2000)	61	12	26	68	10	20
West Virginia (2009)	94	3	1	94	4	1

Note: Figures are rounded to nearest whole numbers.

[a]Percent of drivers
[b]Percent of drivers searched for each race/ethnicity
[c]Percent of all drivers stopped for each race/ethnicity

Percent of Stops Searched by Race/Ethnicity				Percent Yield			
White	Black	Hispanic	Minority	White	Black	Hispanic	Minority
8	3	10		50	43	38	
73[b]	23[b]						
1	2	2		24	—	—	16
3	7	10		43	40	27	
5	6	14		23	22	13	
13	3	9		24	11	9	
7	12	14		20	17	14	
3	5	7					
36[b]	46[b]			23	35		
4			10	24			19
8[b]	7[b]	12		25	28	15	
3	5	6		22	38	39	
4	11	10		47	43	30	

NOTES

1. ACLU and Rights Working Group (2009). *The Persistence of Racial and Ethnic Profiling in the United States 40*; Racial Profiling Data Collection Center at Northeastern University. (n.d.) *Legislation and Litigation.* Retrieved from http://www.racialprofilinganalysis.neu.edu.

2. ACLU and Rights Working Group (2009). *The Persistence of Racial and Ethnic Profiling in the U.S.*

3. Testimony of Melanca D. Clark: Hearing before the General Court of the Commonwealth of Massachusetts Joint Committee on the Judiciary, October 27, 2009.

5

TRAFFIC VIOLATOR
SURVEYS

As increased attention has been focused on racial profiling over the past two decades several methods have been employed to measure the traffic stop phenomenon. A key issue is whether the number of tickets received by black motorists is a fair representation of their driving activities. In other words, when blacks receive a disproportionate rate of tickets to their proportion of the population, does it represent a disproportionate share of traffic violations? Answering this question requires good estimates of the numerator (stops, tickets, etc.,) and the denominator (drivers, violators, etc.).

DEVELOPMENTS IN MEASURING TRAFFIC TICKETING

Along with the emergence of racial profiling as an issue of growing public discussion and debate, research in this area has also evolved rapidly.[1] Researchers have used a variety of methods to collect, analyze, and interpret data regarding the issue of racial profiling. The majority of studies in this area have analyzed racial demographic data recorded on traffic tickets administered within a particular jurisdiction as an indicator of racial profiling or as a proxy for differential law enforcement practices based on the race of the subject, in general. Most of these studies have compared the traffic tickets administered to motorists of different racial groups within a given geographic area or jurisdiction with the racial demographic data for persons in that particular geographic area or jurisdiction eligible to be stopped and ticketed by law enforcement.

The issue of how to define and measure this population against which the racial traffic ticketing data within a particular jurisdiction is to be compared, or what is referred to by researchers as "benchmarking," is a major point of contention among scholars regarding the investigation of racial profiling. Smith and Alpert make a distinction between traffic observation data collected specifically for the purpose of comparison to traffic ticketing data, which they refer to as "baseline data," and the use of preexisting data e.g. Census and Department of Motor Vehicle (DMV) data, as the benchmark to compare against traffic ticketing data.

These researchers refer to the use of direct observation data as the best method of developing a reliable estimate of the driving population.[2] In two of the earliest empirical investigations of racial profiling, John Lamberth compared observational traffic data collected along sections of Interstate 95 (I-95) in New Jersey and Maryland with traffic ticketing data for citations written by the respective state highway patrol in the observation areas in both states.[3] Lamberth conducted a traffic survey in the observation areas, noting the number of "black" motorists and the state on the vehicles' license plates, which was used as the benchmark to define the racial composition of the driving population in studies conducted in each state. The percentage of motorists from each racial group observed speeding was then compared to the percentage of tickets administered to members of each racial group in the areas of the interstate under investigation. These figures were then compared to the percentage of the observed driving population and the statistical population of contiguous states (to both New Jersey and Maryland) that each racial group represented. Using these methods, in New Jersey Lamberth found that blacks represented 13.5 percent of the driving population which was consistent with census data for the eleven states which the majority of the cars observed were registered in, 15 percent of the observed speeders, and yet 46.2 percent of those ticketed and 73.2 percent of those arrested in areas of the interstate under investigation. The findings in Maryland were similar in that blacks in both states were disproportionately being ticketed by the state highway patrol.[4]

In order to account for the influx of the nonresident motorists into a particular jurisdiction some researchers have utilized what are referred to as "gravity models" (see Chapter 3). Social scientists use gravity models to forecast the movement of people, commodities, and information between geographic locations, e.g. cities, counties, etc. Gravity models are based on the notion that "the magnitude of a city's influence on its surrounding hinterland . . . will depend upon . . . the size of the city exerting the influence, and the distance of such city from the affected persons." The influence of the central city is proportional to the city size and inversely related to the distance over which this influence acts.[5]

While the use of a gravity model provides a far-reaching, regional estimate of the driving population it does not provide the demographic precision of the driving population that Harris's use of driving-age and vehicle ownership adjustments affords. The limitations of the research methods used by Lamberth, Harris, and Farrell et al. can be addressed through the use of the gravity model and driving-age and vehicle ownership-adjusted Census data. These integrated methods account for the possibility that any racial disparities found in the analysis of the traffic ticketing data is the result of the disproportionate representation of racial/ethnic groups as residents within the target city and as drivers on the jurisdiction's roadways. It provides a more precise measure of the driving population at risk of being ticketed by police within the designated geographic area. These combined methods provide a rather literal census count of persons of driving-age with access to a motor vehicle within each racial group that are within the region or orbit of the city's gravitational pull and estimated to drive on the city's streets, and thus eligible to be ticketed by police, whereas Harris's use of the driving age only to define the driving population within each racial group accounts for persons of driving age within the city and not from the larger metropolitan region. Nor does Harris account for and reduce the nonblack driving population, which includes whites and other minorities, by the portion of this population that does not have access to a motor vehicle as done for the black driving population. This can lead to an overestimation of the size of the nonblack driving population and distort the magnitude of the disparities observed between racial groups once the driving population data is compared to the actual traffic ticketing data for the jurisdiction.

In other recent studies of racial profiling, researchers working along with the law enforcement agencies examining the issue, have incorporated data collection forms to record information on all stops of citizens by police not only those resulting in a traffic citation.[6] Explicit in the racial profiling argument is the contention that minorities are more heavily scrutinized, stopped or detained, investigated, and penalized by law enforcement than whites. Whereas the use of traffic ticket data provides information regarding those motorists involved in traffic stops that result in a citation it does not provide information on those motorists or stops that result in only a warning or where no citation was written.[7] This is another area within the traffic stop encounter wherein bias can be a considerable factor. The question is whether there is a significant difference, that is, race, between those persons for whom a citation is written and those for whom no record of the stop is documented.[8]

Accordingly, researchers conducting analyses of police–citizen encounters have developed data collection forms that police officers are to complete for all officer-initiated traffic stops, whether a traffic citation is administered or not.[9] Although the information collected on these forms may vary by jurisdiction, in general the basic information obtained should include information regarding the date, time, location, the type of roadway, the reason for the stop, and its duration. Demographic information on the driver such as the race, gender, age, and residence should be included. Information regarding the vehicle's condition, state of registration, and the number of passengers should also be recorded. Information on the outcome of the traffic stop should also be documented, including traffic citation, written warning, arrest made, search of vehicle and/or persons, and any property seized during search.[10]

The data collection form may also include identifying information regarding the police officer involved. This issue is a major point of contention among law enforcement administrators, line officers, and police collective-bargaining units. While each of these groups generally has some degree of apprehension regarding data-collection efforts associated with the examination of racially biased policing practices, the latter two groups are particularly opposed to the inclusion of officer identification data for fear that such data will be used in legal litigation or departmental disciplinary actions against an individual.[11] Police executives are likewise concerned about the use of data that might reflect racial disparities, even that for which legitimate explanations might exist, in legal suits against the agency or municipality.[12]

Once the traffic stop data has been collected the forms are analyzed by racial/ethnic group for each type of traffic stop disposition, such as a citation, written warning, search, arrest, and the like. This data is then compared to the designated benchmark, whether residential Census data or observational traffic data, for the period covered by the study to determine any racial/ethnic disparities in traffic enforcement practices.

A key weakness of the traffic stop data collection forms is the reliance on police officers to collect and accurately record the necessary data on all traffic stops, in spite of their fear that the collection of such data and its usage may not necessarily be in their best interest.[13] In addition, the added paperwork required to complete the traffic stop data collection form is another potential source of contention and problems with the data. In studies conducted in both Cleveland and Richmond, officers' lack of full compliance with the data collection protocol compromised the data. In the Cleveland study, at least one traffic citation was administered in 96.7 percent of the 43,707 reported traffic stops and some other type of official action was taken by police, such as written warning, arrest or search of driver, or one or more passengers in the vehicle, in the majority of the remaining 3.3 percent of the reported traffic stops. It was concluded that officers failed to complete traffic stop forms for all but those stops that resulted in a traffic citation or some other official action.[14] In the Richmond study, it was revealed that officers only completed the data collection forms in 64 percent of the traffic stops. The issue of subject bias or reactivity poses a serious threat to the validity of the data and the credibility of such studies, particularly with the community.[15]

According to Fridell, there are specific alternative hypotheses that researchers using Census data as benchmarks to assess disparities in traffic stops must consider before concluding that disparities in traffic stops/citations are the result of racial bias. She suggests that researchers must account for the possibility of unequal representation of racial/ethnic groups as residents within a jurisdiction, as drivers on jurisdiction roadways, and on roads with high levels of police traffic enforcement activity. She adds that researchers must also account for the possibility that racial/ethnic groups are not equal in their traffic law-violating behavior.[16]

Lamberth's use of benchmark data obtained through direct observation addresses each of Fridell's alternative hypotheses. Harris's methods address only the hypothesis regarding racial/ethnic groups' representation as residents in each jurisdiction, and the presence of only residents, not nonresidents, on the roads. The methods used by Harris do not address the possibility of unequal presence of motorists of different racial/ethnic backgrounds on roads with high-traffic enforcement activity or of exhibiting traffic law-violating behavior. Farrell et al.'s use of the gravity model in conjunction with racial demographic Census data accounted for the presence of racial/ethnic groups as residents in the jurisdiction and as resident and nonresident motorists on jurisdiction roadways. Like Harris's research, this method did not account for differences in racial/ethnic group representation on roads with high traffic enforcement activity or for differences in racial/ethnic groups' violation of traffic laws.

Meehan and Ponder[17] offer an innovative alternative method to address the issue of racial profiling. In order to examine the contention that minorities are disproportionately the subject of unwarranted police surveillance, pretextual stops, and field interrogations and to address the issue of police-initiated traffic stops for which no official record exists, such as a traffic ticket or written warning, Meehan and Ponder analyzed police query data taken from the in-car computers or Mobile Data Terminal (MDT) in police cruisers. This data was used as an indicator of the surveillance and query behavior of police in regard to the driving population. The MDT provides an electronic record of whom the police surveil, the time and location of the query, and what information is requested.[18] The use of MDT data helps address the problem of unrecorded police-initiated stops and interrogations that plague studies which compare traffic ticket data to measures of the driving population. Specially, it helps address the question of whether police are disproportionately focusing on blacks and other minorities as the subject of their surveillance and investigative patrol activities which may or may not result in a stop, whether recorded or not.[19] However, the MDT data does not provide racial demographic data on the individual subject of a police query. Therefore, Meehan and Ponder used the residence of the vehicle owner as a proxy measure for race. These authors argue that the police use a similar mental process based on knowledge of a community's composition that links race and place. These researchers compared the MDT data to the external benchmark data, which they measured by conducting traffic observations in suburban communities characterized by distinct residential segregation patterns, which bordered a city with a large African American population.[20]

In their study, Meehan and Ponder found that African Americans were subjected to significant racial profiling as illustrated in the disproportionate and increasing surveillance and stopping of blacks when driving through whiter neighborhoods, in essence being deemed "out of place."[21] They concluded that profiling is sensitive to race and place and reflects the patterns of residential segregation found in a community.[22] Dunn also found a similar "spatial" effect in his study of racial profiling in the city of Cleveland.[23] There are legal limitations to the use of MDT by nonlaw enforcement personnel in some jurisdictions such as Ohio,[24] where this data is not considered public record as it is in Michigan, the site of Meehan and Ponder's research.

An alternative to the use of external benchmark data—Census, observational, traffic stop data collection forms—to study racial profiling involves the use of internal benchmarks. This method, which Samuel Walker describes as a promising but unproven tool, uses departmental police traffic stop data to compare the traffic enforcement patterns of officers under the same or similar working conditions. The traffic stop, citation, search, and arrest patterns of one officer is compared to that of their peers working the same shift, and comparable patrol areas in order to note any disparities in enforcement practices relative to minorities.[25] According to Walker, this approach addresses the issue of determining the appropriate benchmark to assess racial disparities in traffic enforcement, which plague studies using census data or other external benchmarks, by comparing the relevant internal departmental data to identify officers that stop a disproportionate number of minorities relative to their counterparts.

While this method holds potential for identifying officers that exhibit patterns of disproportionately targeting minorities for law enforcement actions, it fails to address institutional-level racism wherein departments or agencies exhibit patterns of racial bias in enforcement practices.[26] In addition, the internal benchmark data as described by Walker is part of a comprehensive personnel assessment system or an "early intervention" (EI) system which is used to identify officers whose performance records reflect patterns that are reason for concern. Although the use of EI systems are recommended by the U.S. Civil Rights Commission as a means of identifying problematic officers and are now recognized as a "best practice in policing" by the Department of Justice (DOJ) and is required for all departments entering settlements with the DOJ in pattern or practice suits, EI systems have not been adopted by all large agencies as suggested by the Commission on Accreditation for Law Enforcement Agencies.[27]

As mentioned above, direct observation data appears to be the best method of developing reliable estimates of the driving population. Lamberth used the observational approach in his early studies of racial profiling.[28] His use of benchmark data obtained through observation resolves the issues raised by Fridell,[29] who argued that researchers must account for unequal representation of racial/ethnic groups as residents within a jurisdiction, as drivers on jurisdiction roadways, and on roads with high levels of police traffic enforcement activity. She also specified that researchers must account for the possibility that racial/ethnic groups are not equal in their traffic law-violating behavior. The observational approach handles those issues. We use that method in the following examination of traffic ticketing practices.

OBSERVATIONAL STUDIES

To assess racial differentials in speeding and ticketing, we generated two additional sets of data. The first of these two data sets was generated from a traffic census conducted along the two thoroughfares under investigation—one with a majority white driving population and one with a predominantly black driving population. Three thousand nine hundred fifty-four (3,954) traffic observations were recorded, noting only the race of the driver of motor vehicles using these streets during the designated observation times.

The second of these two data sets contains two samples of speed recordings from the observation sites. There were 2,015 speed recordings taken on both thoroughfares. On Kinsman Road where the speed limit varied between 35 and 25 mph 491 speed recordings were taken in a 25-mph zone. The speed limit along Chester was constant at 35 mph. These records include the speed and race of the motorists, the street, the direction of travel (east–west), and the time of day (morning/evening).

The traffic survey was conducted along Kinsman Road and Chester Avenue, Monday through Friday, from 7–9 a.m. during the morning rush hour and 4–6 p.m. during the evening rush hour. The traffic census counted the race of motorists using these thoroughfares during the same hours. The traffic census data was used to determine the percentage black and white motorists utilizing each traffic artery.

The racial categories used in the traffic surveys were the same as those used by the Cleveland Police Department to identify the race of motorists: black, white, and unknown.[30] Those motorists identified as unknown and all other racial groups were categorized as "other." Visual observations of motorists' skin complexion and phenotype were used to determine race. Those cases in which a motorist's features were obscured by heavily tinted windows or sun glare were discarded from the surveys.

Traffic Ticket/Traffic Census Data Analyzed by Race and Street

The traffic census data were analyzed to determine the percentage of motorists of each race using Chester Avenue and Kinsman Road during rush hour. Ticket data from the traffic ticket database were then sorted by race for the two specific thoroughfares under investigation and the number of motorists of each race ticketed was compared to the number from each racial group observed speeding in the traffic violator survey data. Data from the traffic census and violator survey were also compared to the traffic ticket data to compute ticket to driving population ratios, and likelihood ratios for each racial group on the observed arterial routes.

Westbound traffic heading toward downtown Cleveland on the city's Eastside was observed in the morning and eastbound traffic heading toward the suburbs was observed in the evening. The 3,954 traffic census observations were collected between the sites during the late summer and the early fall (August to October) to account for differences in the driving population when school was out of session as well as in session. A total of 18 observation hours were spent at each site.

There were 1,894 traffic census observations of eastbound and westbound traffic collected along Chester Avenue during the morning and evening rush hours, of which whites were 60.5 percent of the driving population, blacks were 37.2 percent, and persons of other races were 2.4 percent of the motorists. Of the 2,060 traffic census observations collected along Kinsman during both morning and evening rush hours blacks represented 93.2 percent of the driving population, while whites made up 6.5 percent, and persons of other races were less than 1 percent (0.4 percent) of the motorists.

Blacks were the recipients of 61 percent of the traffic tickets written on Chester while whites received 34 percent and motorists of other races accounted for 5 percent of the traffic citations. Meanwhile, on Kinsman blacks received 90 percent of the traffic tickets compared to 9 percent received by whites and 1 percent going to persons of other races (see Table 5.1).

Comparing the percentage of tickets received by each racial group to their percentage of the driving population on each traffic artery reveals that blacks were disproportionately ticketed on Chester as they garnered 61 percent of the tickets yet were 37 percent of the driving population. Computed as a ratio, blacks received 1.64 or 164 percent of their proportional share of tickets on Chester (Table 5.1). Whites, on the other hand, received 34 percent of the traffic citations and were 61 percent of the driving population on Chester, meaning they received just over half (0.56) of their proportional share of tickets on this major traffic artery. Motorists of other races accounted for 5 percent of those ticketed and were 2.4 percent of the driving population on Chester.

TABLE 5.1 Traffic Ticket/Traffic Census Data by Race and Street

Traffic Artery	Race	Tickets Received	Percentage of Tickets	Traffic Census (DP)	% Tickets/DP Ratio
Chester	Black	1,024	61%	37.2%	1.64
	White	579	34%	60.5%	0.56
	Other	79	5%	2.4%	2.1
	Total	1,682	100%	100%	—
Kinsman	Black	5,720	90%	93.2%	0.97
	White	553	9%	6.5%	1.38
	Other	93	1%	0.4%	2.5
	Total	6,366	100%	100%	—

Note: DP = driving population.

While the negligible number of members of this group observed in the driving population might distort the comparisons relative to this group, there was a positive 2.6 percentage point disparity between the portion of the driving population they represented and the percentage of tickets they received, meaning motorists of other races received 2.1 times or 210 percent of their proportional share of tickets on Chester.[31]

The disparity in ticketing and percentage of driving population was not as acute on Kinsman for blacks, as the percentage of the driving population they represent and the percentage of traffic tickets they received were almost equal at 93 percent and 90 percent respectively. Blacks received slightly less than their proportional share of traffic citations on Kinsman. Whites traveling on Kinsman received 138 percent of their proportional share of tickets as they were 6.5 percent of the driving population and received 9 percent of the tickets. This means whites received more than their proportional share of tickets on Kinsman. Motorists of other races were 0.4 of a percent of the driving population on Kinsman and received 1 percent of the traffic tickets written there. Thus, minority drivers of other races received 2.5 times their proportional share of tickets on Kinsman.

Table 5.2 shows the distribution of tickets, the ticket to driving population ratios, and the likelihood ratios across the two years, from the middle of 1999 to the middle of 2001. Except for 2001 on Kinsman, the data are consistent across the years. In 2001 blacks were only one-third as likely as whites to be ticketed on Kinsman. Contrastingly, they were almost 30 percent *more* likely to be ticketed on Kinsman in 1999 and 2000. On Chester they were 2.64 times to 3.47 times as likely as whites to be ticketed.

Violator Survey Data Analyzed by Race and Street

A radar gun using the same Doppler Radar technology used by law enforcement was used to determine those motorists violating the posted speed limit along Chester and Kinsman.[32] In order to record motorists' speed yet avoid creating Hawthorne Effects on driving behavior, the investigator was positioned in the most inconspicuous vantage point possible (e.g., in car parked on side street perpendicular to approaching traffic, at intersection, glass bus stop shelter, behind trees, bushes, etc.) while conducting these observations. A total of 2,015 speed readings were collected between the two thoroughfares—1,050 on Chester and 965 on Kinsman, including 491 in the 25-mph zone.

The speed of the first vehicle to approach the investigator's vantage point was recorded. After clocking and recording the speed and race of the driver of the first vehicle on a survey log, the radar gun was reset and the speed of the next observed vehicle to approach the observation point was recorded.

TABLE 5.2 Traffic Census/Traffic Ticket Data by Race, Street, and Year

Traffic Artery		Traffic Census (DP)	Tickets Received			Ticket/DP Ratio			Likelihood Ratio*		
			1999	2000	2001	1999	2000	2001	1999	2000	2001
Black	Chester	37.2%	66%	61%	60%	1.77	1.63	1.61	3.47	2.91	2.64
	Kinsman	93.2%	94%	94%	80%	1.0	1.0	0.86	1.29	1.29	0.31
White	Chester	60.5%	31%	34%	37%	0.51	0.56	0.61	—	—	—
	Kinsman	6.5%	5%	5%	18%	0.77	0.77	2.77	—	—	—
Other[1]	Chester	2.4%	3%	5%	3%	1.25	2.08	1.25	2.45	3.71	2.05
	Kinsman	0.4%	1%	1%	2%	2.5	2.5	5	3.25	3.25	1.81

*Whites were used as the comparison reference group for blacks and others to compute the Likelihood Ratio.

[1]The small percentage of persons of other races included in the traffic census sample significantly inflates their Ticket-to-Driving Population and Likelihood Ratios.

It took approximately 30 seconds to record each observation, reset the radar, and prepare to record the next observation. This represents a randomized selection process in that it is systematic, and all motorists using these thoroughfares during the observation period had an equal chance of being included in the sample. As the traffic generally flowed in intervals due to traffic light sequencing, the first to approach the observation point and be recorded was typically the one traveling at the highest rate of speed. The subsequent observations recorded were of those vehicles traveling at a lesser rate of speed, thus providing a representative sample of speeds and motorists.

Whites were 57 percent all motorists driving above the 35 mph speed limit on Chester, a rate slightly less than their 60 percent of the driving population on that street; while blacks were 40 percent of the speeders over 35 mph, compared to their 37.2 percent of the driving population (Table 5.3). Blacks were the predominant race using Kinsman and they were the predominant group exceeding the 35 mph speed limit. They were 93.2 percent of the driving population and 93 percent of the speeders.

It is a common belief that the police generally will not give a person a ticket for speeding unless they are traveling 10 mph or more above the speed limit. For that reason, percentages were also calculated for speeders traveling 10 mph or more above the posted 35 mph (equal or greater than 45 mph) and 25 mph (equal or greater than 35 mph) speed limit in each zone. Blacks represented 36 percent of the motorists traveling 45 mph or more on Chester, while whites were 59 percent, and other minorities were 5 percent. Blacks on Kinsman were 91 percent of those driving 45 mph or higher, and one white motorist represented the other nine percent. Within the 25-mph zone on Kinsman, blacks were 93 percent of those traveling 35 mph or more, and whites constituted the remaining 7 percent.

Using the 10 mph or more measure to analyze the violator survey data reveals that more whites and other minorities drove 45 mph or higher on Chester than blacks. In the 25-mph zones on Kinsman, the opposite was observed as the proportion of black motorists traveling in excess of 10 mph above the speed limit equaled their proportion of the driving population. No motorists of other races exceeded the 25-mph speed limit on Kinsman by 10 mph or more. These results support the earlier findings that whites and other minority motorists drive faster than blacks on Chester, and blacks drive faster than both groups on Kinsman.

Therefore, it can be concluded that traffic on Chester travels at a higher rate of speed than traffic on Kinsman. Also, the majority of motorists on Chester and those driving within 25-mph zones on Kinsman exceeded the posted speed limits, while the average speed of all motorists within 35-mph zones

TABLE 5.3 Traffic Census and Violator Survey Observations by Street and Race

Traffic Artery	Race	Traffic Census		35 mph zone				25 mph zone			
				All Speeders		Driving 45+ mph*		All Speeders		Driving 35+ mph*	
		N	%	N	%	N	%	N	%	N	%
Chester	Black	704	37.2%	380	40%	45	36%	—	—	—	—
	White	1,145	60.5%	548	57%	74	59%	—	—	—	—
	Other	45	2.4%	32	3%	7	5%	—	—	—	—
	Total	1,894	100%	960	100%	126	100%	—	—	—	—
Kinsman	Black	1,919	93.2%	281	93%	10	91%	361	90.25%	126	93%
	White	133	6.5%	22	7%	1	9%	38	9.5%	10	7%
	Other	8	0.4%	—	—	—	—	1	0.25%	—	—
	Total	2,060	100%	303	100%	11	100%	400	100%	136	100%

*Rates were computed for violators in excess of 10 mph or more above the speed limit for each speed zone in that it is believed that 10 mph above the speed limit is the threshold at which police will ticket motorists.

on Kinsman were below the speed limit. In general, whites drive at a higher rate of speed than blacks on Chester where whites are the majority, and blacks drive faster than whites on Kinsman where blacks are the majority of the driving population. Motorists of other races drive faster than both groups on Chester; however, these figures might not be representative given the small number of other minorities observed in the driving population.

Blacks on Chester drove an average of 38.52 mph compared to whites who had an average speed of 39.75 mph. All of the observations for other minority motorists occurred on Chester, therefore their average speed is the 41.16 mph reported earlier. Within the 35-mph zones on Kinsman, the average speed for black motorists was 33.38 mph while whites averaged 30.63 mph. This data shows that blacks drove at a higher rate of speed in the 35-mph zones on Kinsman than whites, and whites drove faster than blacks on Chester, while members of other racial groups drove faster than both blacks and whites on Chester (Table 5.4).

Comparing the percentage of speeders of each race exceeding the 35 mph speed limit on each thoroughfare with the percentage of tickets distributed to motorists of each race on the respective streets over the two-year observation period reveals a disparity between the number of tickets blacks received and the percentage of black speeders on Chester. Whites received only 34.2 percent

TABLE 5.4 Average Speeds by Race and Street

Race	Traffic Artery	Avg. Speed 35 mph zones	Standard Deviation	Avg. Speed 25 mph zones	Standard Deviation
All Motorists	Both Streets	37.82	5.72	—	—
	Chester	39.34	—	—	—
	Kinsman	33	—	32.53	4.59
Black	Both Streets	36.24	1.46	—	—
	Chester	38.52	—	—	—
	Kinsman	33.38	—	32.7	4.62
White	Both Streets	39.47	0.48	—	—
	Chester	39.75	—	—	—
	Kinsman	30.63	—	31	4.03
Other	Both Streets	—	—	—	—
	Chester	41.16	4.4	—	—
	Kinsman	—	—	27*	—

*Only one motorist of another race was observed in a 25 mph zone.

of the tickets written on Chester, yet represented 57 percent of the observed speeders on the artery. Motorists of other races were 4.9 percent of those ticketed on Chester and accounted for 3 percent of those speeding. Therefore, based on this comparative analysis of the violator data with the traffic ticket data, blacks and other minority motorists were over-ticketed on Chester while whites were under-ticketed on this thoroughfare.

Blacks were 93 percent of the speeders observed on Kinsman and were 90 percent of those ticketed there. In comparison, whites represented 7 percent of the observed speeders on Kinsman, and were 9 percent of those ticketed on Kinsman. As stated earlier, no motorists of other races were observed speeding during the violator survey, therefore no data are available to compare with the 1.2 percent of tickets this group received on Kinsman. Based on the violator and traffic ticket data comparative analysis, blacks on Kinsman received 3.2 percent (0.03/0.93) less than the amount of tickets they should have received, and whites received 28.6 percent (0.02/0.07) more tickets than their portion of the speeding population on Kinsman would warrant.

The *ticket to speeder ratio* in Table 5.5 represents the ratio of the percentage of tickets received by each race divided by their percentage among the population of speeders observed on each thoroughfare. Blacks on Chester had a ticket to speeder ratio of 1.52 while whites had a ticket to speeder ratio of 0.60. With 1.0 representing equilibrium, this means blacks received over 50 percent more tickets than they should have received given the 40 percent of speeders they represented on Chester, while whites received 40 percent fewer tickets than they should have received given their 57 percent among speeders. Motorists of other races had a ticket to speeder ratio of 1.26 on

TABLE 5.5   Violator Survey/Traffic Ticket Data

		Traffic Census (DP)	Average Speed	Tickets Received (Cum.)	Violator Survey Speeders	Ticket/ Speeders Ratio	Likelihood Ratio*
Black	Chester	37.2%	38.52	60.7%	40%	1.52	2.53
	Kinsman	93.2%	33.38	90%	93%	0.97	0.76
White	Chester	60.5%	39.75	34.2%	57%	0.60	0.39
	Kinsman	6.5%	30.63	9%	7%	1.28	1.32
Other	Chester	2.4%	41.16	4.9%	3.9%	1.26	2.10
	Kinsman	0.4%	—	1.2%	—	—	—

*Whites were used as the comparison reference group for blacks and others to compute the Likelihood Ratio; and blacks were used as the comparison reference group for whites.

Chester, receiving 26 percent more tickets than expected relative to their portion of the speeders on this thoroughfare. Blacks on Kinsman had a ticket to speeder ratio of 0.97, while whites had a ticket to speeder ratio of 1.28, meaning that blacks received close to their proportionate number of tickets, while whites received 28 percent more than their share. No motorists of other races were observed on Kinsman during the violator survey, therefore there is no comparative data. There was very little difference between the percentage of motorists from each racial group among the speeding population and their percentages in the overall driving populations on both thoroughfares.

A *likelihood ratio* was computed for blacks and other minorities by dividing each group's ticket to speeder ratio on each thoroughfare by that of whites. This figure tells the likelihood of nonwhite motorists being ticketed in comparison to whites. A likelihood ratio of one means that group received its proportional share of traffic tickets in relation to that of the reference group. Based on these calculations, blacks were 2.53 times as likely to be ticketed on Chester Avenue as whites, and other minorities were 2.10 (1.26/0.60) times as likely to be ticketed on Chester as whites.

Although the ticketing of blacks on Kinsman was close to equilibrium, they were three-fourths (0.76) as likely as whites to be ticketed on that street. In that whites are disproportionately ticketed on Kinsman in relation to their percentage among the speeding population on Kinsman, a ticket to speeder ratio was computed for whites using blacks as the reference group. It revealed that whites are 1.32 (1.28/0.97) times as likely to be ticketed on Kinsman as blacks and received 32 percent more than their proportional share of tickets relative to their proportion of the speeding population on Kinsman.

SUMMARY AND DISCUSSION

Motorists on the street with predominantly black motorists, Kinsman, were more frequently sanctioned for traffic violations than motorists traveling on the majority white driver thoroughfare, Chester. Although Kinsman had more than 5,000 fewer vehicles per day than Chester, drivers on Kinsman received nearly four times the number of tickets as drivers on Chester.

Given the predominantly black driving population on Kinsman the overwhelming majority of those ticketed on this street were black. While blacks on Kinsman were ticketed at approximately the same rate as their proportion of drivers on this street, they were disproportionately ticketed on Chester, the street with the majority of white drivers. Blacks received two-thirds more tickets on Chester than their proportion of the driving population, compared to near parity on Kinsman.

Drivers on Kinsman were ticketed substantially more often than drivers on Chester, despite the fact that more drivers exceeded the speed limits on

Chester. The speeds on Chester averaged above the speed limit, while on Kinsman they averaged below the speed limit. While both blacks and whites on Chester drove at speeds averaging above the speed limit, the rate of speed of black motorists was lower than that of white motorists. Despite being fewer drivers and driving at lower speeds, blacks received more tickets than whites on Chester. On Kinsman, white drivers received tickets at a rate greater than their proportion of the population.

Thus, where the race of the driver is in the minority of the races using the thoroughfare, such drivers tend to receive tickets in excess of their proportion of the population, or their proportion of the speeders. While whites suffer this phenomenon, it is to a lesser extent than blacks. Substantially more important is the attention paid to thoroughfares used predominantly by blacks.

NOTES

1. M. R. Smith, & G. P. Alpert (2002). "Searching for Direction: Courts, Social Science, and the Adjudication of Racial Profiling Claims." *Justice Quarterly 19*, (4).

2. Ibid.

3. J. Lamberth (1996). *State of New Jersey v. Pedro Soto*, 324 N. J. Super. 66; 734 A.2d 350; 1996 N. J. Super. Lexis 554.

4. Ibid.; D, Harris, *Profiles in Injustice: Why Racial Profiling Cannot Work* (New York: The New Press, 2002).

5. J. D. Carroll (1955). Spatial Interactions and the Urban-Metropolitan Description. *Traffic Quarterly,* 149–161.

6. J. Liderbach, C. R. Trulson, E. J. Fritsch, T. J. Caeti, & R. W. Taylor (2007). Racial Profiling and the Political Demand for Data: A Pilot Study Designed to Improve Methodologies in Texas. *Criminal Justice Review 32*(2): pp. 101–120; R. S. Engel, J. Frank, R. Tillyer, & C. Klahm (2006). *Cleveland Division of Police Traffic Stop Data Study: Final Report.* Cincinnati: University of Cincinnati, Division of Criminal Justice; L. A. Fridell, R. Lunney, D. Diamond, B. Kubu, M. Scott, & C. Laing (2001). Racially Biased Policing: A Principled Response. Washington, D. C.: Police Executive Research Forum.

7. Harris, *Profiles in Injustice*, 2002; L. A. Fridell (2004). By the Numbers: A Guide for Analyzing Race Data from Vehicle Stops. Washington, D.C.: Police Executive Research Forum.

8. M. R. Smith, & G. P. Alpert (2002). "Searching for Direction: Courts, Social Science, and the Adjudication of Racial Profiling Claims," *Justice Quarterly 19* (4).

9. Engel, et al., *Cleveland Division of Police Traffic Stop Data Study*; Fridell, *By the Numbers*.

10. Fridell, et al., *Racially Biased Policing*; Smith and Alpert, *Searching for Direction*.

11. Engel, et al., *Cleveland Division of Police Traffic Stop Data Study*; D. A. Harris, A. David. *Good Cop: The Case for Preventive Policing* (New York: The New Press, 2005);

Fridell, et al., *Racially Biased Policing*; S. Walker. *Police Accountability: The Role of Citizen Oversight* (Belmont, CA: Wadsworth Group, 2001).

12. Fridell, et al., *Racially Biased Policing*.

13. Engel, et al., *Cleveland Division of Police Traffic Stop Data Study*; Fridell, et al., *Racially Biased Policing*; D. Ramirez, J. McDevitt, & A. Farrell. *A Resource Guide on Racial Profiling Data Collection Systems* (Boston: Northeastern University, 2000).

14. Engel, et al., *Cleveland Division of Police Traffic Stop Data Study*.

15. M. R. Smith, & M. Petrocelli (2001). "Racial Profiling? A Multivariate Analysis of Police Traffic Stop Data," *Police Quarterly 4*: pp. 4–27.

16. Fridell, *By the Numbers*.

17. A. J. Meehan, & M. C. Ponder (2002). Race and Place: The Ecology of Racial Profiling African American Motorists, *Justice Quarterly 19* (3): pp. 401–430.

18. Ibid.

19. Ibid.

20. Ibid.

21. Ibid, p. 422.

22. Ibid.

23. R. A. Dunn (2004). "Spatial Profiling: To What Extent Do the Cleveland Police Department's Traffic Ticketing Patterns Disproportionately Target Blacks?" (Doctoral Dissertation, Cleveland State University, 2004; UMI No. 072699).

24. This is according to a lieutenant with the Ohio Highway Patrol which administers the Mobile Data Terminal data as told to Dunn and colleagues in an effort to use the MDT data to replicate Meehan & Ponders study in Cleveland and a number of surrounding suburban jurisdictions in December, 2009.

25. S. Walker (March, 2003). *Internal Benchmarking for Traffic Stop Data: An Early Intervention System Approach.* Paper presented at the conference, Confronting Racial Profiling in the 21st Century, Boston, MA.; S. Walker, S. *The New World of Police Accountability* (London: Sage Publications, 2005).

26. Walker, *The New World of Police Accountability*.

27. Ibid.

28. Lamberth, *State of NJ v. Pedro Soto*.

29. Fridell, *By the Numbers*.

30. Information gathered from discussion with Cleveland Police Department traffic ticket database administrator.

31. It is plausible that a considerable portion of other minority motorists that might utilize Chester to commute to the Cleveland Clinic might have exited Chester prior to reaching the observation points.

32. The investigator received general instructions on use of a radar gun from a member of the Cleveland police department as well as the instructions that came with the equipment.

6

INSTITUTIONAL PRACTICES AND INSTITUTIONAL RACISM

The analysis of traffic ticket data from the city of Cleveland for a two-year period using gravity model estimates of the city's driving population revealed that blacks were disproportionately ticketed by the Cleveland police department (CPD) relative to their presence in the city's driving population. Blacks driving on city streets received almost one and a half times (1.45) their proportional share of traffic tickets and were more than twice as likely (2.13) to be ticketed by police as white motorists. Although minority motorists of other races received less than their proportional share of tickets citywide (0.86) they were roughly one and one-fourth (1.26) times as likely to be ticketed as whites. Whites driving in the city received considerably less than their share of tickets (0.68) relative to their proportion of the driving population.

A comparative analysis of traffic ticket distribution by race within the context of the racial demographics of the city's six police districts revealed that blacks received considerably more tickets than their percentage of the population in four police districts. Three of the districts where blacks received a disproportionate share of tickets were located on the predominately white Westside and the other was in the district on the predominately black Eastside with the largest percentage of white residents (29.6 percent). Minority motorists of other races were disproportionately ticketed in all six police districts, and whites received more than their proportional share of tickets in two Eastside police districts. And observational traffic surveys along two major Eastside, inner-city, traffic arteries used by two racially prominent driving populations to commute to and from the central business district during rush hours revealed that while the majority of all motorists (76 percent) exceed the posted speed limits, the speed limit was more strictly enforced on the road used by the predominately black driving population than on the traffic artery used primarily by white motorists.

To the extent that the speed limit was enforced on the artery with the predominately white driving population, blacks and other minorities were disproportionately ticketed relative to their percentage of this driving population. Conversely, whites and other minorities were disproportionately ticketed on the thoroughfare used by the predominately black driving population.[1]

Aside from the higher average speeds of blacks on Kinsman and other minorities and whites on Chester in the violator survey, there is nothing in the data, nor in the research literature to suggest that, in general, members of one particular racial group violate traffic laws more than members of any other racial group. Therefore, all else being equal, one would expect to find roughly the same percentage of motorists from each racial group among those receiving traffic tickets as their percentage of the driving population.

TICKETING PRACTICES

This study's findings that blacks are disproportionately ticketed for traffic violations in the city of Cleveland are consistent with Harris's findings in the four major Ohio cities included in his study: Columbus/Franklin County, Akron, Toledo, and Dayton. The citywide racial disparity in ticketing of blacks in Cleveland is actually greater than those found in these other Ohio cities as shown in Table 6.1.

Even using Harris's racial categories grouping whites with motorists of all other races and comparing blacks and nonblacks, blacks in Cleveland still have a greater likelihood of being ticketed[2] than blacks in the other cities.

TABLE 6.1 Likelihood of Blacks Being Ticketed in Major Ohio Cities

City	Likelihood Ratio for Blacks
Cleveland	2.13
	(2.07)*
Columbus/Franklin County	1.8
Akron	2.04
Toledo	2.02
Dayton	1.8

*Likelihood ratio of black motorists being ticketed using nonblack measurement (see endnote 2).

This finding not only illustrates that DWB is a problem in Cleveland and the magnitude of the disproportionate ticketing of blacks in the city, it also bolsters Harris's overall conclusion that "a driving while black problem does indeed exist in Ohio."[3]

The violator survey findings exemplify the inconsistencies in the Cleveland police department's (CPD's) enforcement of traffic laws between the races as whites were 57 percent of the observed speeders on Chester Avenue but received only 34 percent of the tickets written on that thoroughfare while blacks were 40 percent of the speeders on Chester yet received 61 percent of the tickets. Meanwhile, traffic laws appeared to be enforced by a different, more objective standard on Kinsman where blacks were 93 percent of the observed speeders and 90 percent of those ticketed and whites were 7 percent of those speeding and 9 percent of those ticketed.

The under-ticketing of whites on Chester, and the over-ticketing of blacks on Chester and whites on Kinsman in relation to each groups' percentage of the respective driving populations suggest that police discretion is in part responsible for the observed differences in ticketing between the races. The impact of police discretion on ticketing patterns is evident in the traffic ticket data from the period of the work slowdown initiated by police in response to the then-mayor's investigation of racism in the CPD in 1999, where 30 to 75 percent decreases in ticketing were recorded in some neighborhoods.[4] The disparity in the racial distribution of tickets on Chester indicate that white motorists using Chester were given what Wilbanks[5] refers to as a "break" by the police as whites were not cited at the level that their percentage of the driving population or among the observed speeders in the violator survey would suggest.

While police discretion might explain some of the racial disparities in ticketing observed among the driving populations on these thoroughfares, it is highly improbable that the discretion of individual patrol officers accounts for the disparity found in ticketing between the two traffic arteries. As noted, the volume of traffic is heavier on Chester, a six-lane roadway, than along Kinsman, a four-lane artery, as 57,929 motorists use Chester daily while 52,875 motorists use Kinsman. Thus, 10 percent (5,054) more motorists use Chester each day than use Kinsman. The results of the violator survey also found that traffic travels at a higher rate of speed on Chester as 81 percent of the motorists drive above the 35 mph speed limit, compared to 69 percent of all motorists that exceed the posted speed limit on Kinsman (33 percent in 35 mph and 95 percent in 25 mph speed zones). Despite these findings that clearly indicate there is a higher frequency of speeding and thus a need for increased speed limit enforcement on Chester, 4,684 more traffic tickets were written on Kinsman.

These factors show that traffic ticket writing activities are concentrated along the thoroughfare primarily used by black motorists in comparison to that used primarily by whites commuting to and from the eastern suburbs to the downtown area, but they also support the contention that the racial disparities in the traffic ticketing patterns in the city of Cleveland are attributable to institutional racism within the Cleveland police department.

DEPARTMENTAL PRACTICE

The former mayor's investigation of the police department concluded that there was no evidence of "organized" racist activity within the Cleveland police department. If the 4,684 difference in ticketing between the two thoroughfares had resulted from the conscious, collective use of police discretion, this would clearly constitute "organized racist activity," which should have come to the attention of investigators. In that such activities were not found, it is reasonable to conclude that the disparity in the volume of tickets between the two thoroughfares is not the result of the discretion of individual police officers working in concert, but rather a reflection of police deployment patterns.

According to former city safety director Henry Guzman, traffic ticket distribution patterns represent police traffic enforcement assignments or deployment patterns in that, "we set up assignments based upon concerns that people raise or based on accidents. If an area is prone to accidents or when there have been violations of traffic signals or stop signs we will target for enforcement."[6] Thus, the traffic ticket distribution patterns observed in this study are taken as a reflection of police deployment patterns.

Based on the safety director's explanation of traffic enforcement deployment patterns one would expect to find a higher occurrence of accidents on Kinsman than Chester; however an analysis of the traffic ticket database does not support his claim. During the study period 2 percent (129) of the tickets administered on Kinsman (6,366) were to vehicles involved in traffic accidents, while two and four-tenths percent (40) of the tickets written on Chester (1,682) were to vehicles involved in an accident. Given the slightly higher percentage of accidents that occurred on Chester, the deployment patterns must be based on the higher number of traffic violations on Kinsman. This creates a self-fulfilling prophecy in that more police officers are deployed on Kinsman and in turn write more tickets thereby justifying their heightened presence in the area. And although CPD and city public safety officials have readily denied or dismissed any allegations of racially biased traffic law enforcement practices, the patterns found in the traffic ticket data suggest otherwise.[7]

Policies governing police department resources and procedures including traffic law enforcement are generally communicated within the department and districts through General Police Orders (GPO), and departmental and district directives.[8] The deployment of traffic law enforcement patrols is usually established at the district level. This is not to say that the patterns of disproportionate ticketing of blacks found in the city are the result of intentional racially discriminatory policies, but rather a reflection of institutionalized practices manifested in the deployment patterns. As Jones states,[9] "race-conscious intentionality is not a prerequisite for institutional racism." In fact, the Cleveland police department's policy governing citizen stops appears to be a "bias-free"[10] policy as its purpose is "to ensure proactive enforcement and fair treatment of citizens,"[11] and it explicitly admonishes against stopping persons based solely on their race along with other sociodemographic characteristics. The policy states:

Members of the Division of Police shall be vigilant and take appropriate enforcement action. Stopping a citizen constitutes a seizure. Members shall not stop a person only due to the person's race, ethnicity, religion, gender, or sexual orientation. Members shall treat all persons with proper courtesy and dignity, and shall speak and act professionally. Officers shall not stop a person without the ability to articulate the suspicion for the stop.[12]

The policy also includes the procedures that officers are to follow when conducting a stop, and the objectives of a traffic stop, which are to:

A. Interrupt an ongoing violation of law;
B. Prevent traffic crashes and hazardous conditions;
C. Have a symbolic effect on other traffic; a police car with a violator pulled over demonstrates to the public that the police are visibly on patrol;
D. Detect evidence of a more serious violation; and
E. Have a positive effect on the motorist's future driving behavior by acting in a professional manner.

And although the department's policy on traffic stops would not be considered "race-conscious," the institutional practices that emanate from it can and does have "race effects"[13] as exhibited in the traffic ticket distribution patterns observed in the city of Cleveland. As Jones states, "when these race effects are systematically advantaging to whites and disadvantaging to ethnic and racial minority groups, they represent a standard of practice criterion of institutional racism." These standards of practice are "processes that are assumed to be appropriate, fair, and reasonable, but that, nevertheless, are associated with adverse racial results."[14]

The established traffic enforcement deployment patterns along with the existence of an implicit ticketing quota reduce the influence of individual police discretion in ticketing and also minimize the significance of the police officer's race in determining the racial distribution of traffic tickets in the city. Although the city's safety director denied allegations made by the president of the Cleveland Police Patrolman's Association during the 1999 work slowdown that the mayor's coercing "officers to issue multiple citations, each costing about $150, solely to boost revenue and statistics," which he argued "unfairly punishes law-abiding citizens,"[15] is the equivalent of a quota on issuing tickets, the then-chief of police ordered police supervisors to, "start counting the number of arrests and citations officers make," to be used in the officers' yearly performance evaluations,[16] which in essence does convey an implicit quota or ultimatum. Therefore, by merely performing their job in accordance with expected performance measures within the assigned deployment areas police, particularly traffic patrol officers, are compelled to issue a certain amount of traffic tickets regardless of the officer's race or the racial composition of the driving population within the given area of operation. As Anderson states, "in doing their job, the police often become willing parties to this general color-coding of the public environment."[17]

While not totally discounting individual police officers' use of discretion in determining the outcome of the racial distribution of traffic tickets in the city of Cleveland, the traffic enforcement deployment patterns and the implied ticketing quota reduce the significance of the race of the police officer and the relevance of police discretion in this form of racial profiling. However, as noted earlier, individual police discretion or prejudices can and obviously do operate within the parameters of the geographical deployment patterns established at levels above that of the patrol officer, given the racial disparities in ticketing found within the driving populations of the thoroughfares under observation in this study.

Also relevant to the differential traffic law-enforcement practices employed along the observed thoroughfares is the policy statement that "officers of the Division shall enforce laws, and detain suspects *whenever* there is reasonable suspicion that they have committed, are committing, or are about to commit an infraction."[18] This departmental directive calls on officers to enforce the law "whenever" a violation occurs. For the most part, the Cleveland police seem to adhere to the frequency aspect of this edict on Kinsman; however, that does not appear to be the case on Chester.

These differences in the enforcement practices of the CPD are symptomatic of the institutionalized racist standards of practice within the department. Two statements have been made by both current and former CPD officials that support the existence of institutionalized racism within the department. The first is a June 1999 memorandum from then-deputy chief of special operations, Ronald James, to the then-chief of police, Martin Flask, about the use of racial profiling in the department, which was included in the mayor's investigation on racism. In the memorandum James stated, "the Cleveland Division of Police, like most police agencies, especially those that experienced urban insurrections in the 1960's, is rife with 'institutionalized racism.'" James defined institutional racism as:

The collective failure of an organization to provide an appropriate professional service to people because of their color, culture or ethnic origin reflected in processes, attitudes and behavior which amount to discrimination through unwitting prejudice, ignorance, thoughtlessness and racist stereotyping.[19]

The deputy chief went on to identify two categories in which he contends that the CPD practiced "unofficial racial profiling." The first category is representative of the traditional sense of racial profiling or DWB in which he charges that "young, inexperienced officers" identify young African American males as drug dealers and criminals and use pretextual traffic stops "to search for evidence, weapons, and fruits of crime." He states that the officer then issues a ticket to justify the stop.

The deputy chief describes the second category of racial profiling within the department as a situation wherein "officers who make a living preying on the citizens of Cleveland use the issuing of Uniform Traffic Tickets [UTT] as a means of generating personal income." James is referring to the fact that officers receive overtime pay for court appearances. Therefore officers are paid for any traffic tickets they issue that are contested and result in them having to appear in court. Feeling strongly about the existence of this practice the deputy chief added, "although demographics are not currently kept on UTT's, a hand-search would reveal a disproportionate number of minorities receiving tickets."[20] Given the racially segregated characteristics of the city of Cleveland as illustrated by the racial demographics of the city's six police districts, it can be inferred from James's argument that these practices will primarily be concentrated on the city's predominately black Eastside.

And a statement made by retired former Cleveland chief of police, Ed Kovacic, during a 1999 television news investigative report on racial profiling, is instructive in understanding how such institutionalized racist standards of practice that disadvantage blacks in Cleveland have permeated and been transmitted through the department for decades.[21] When asked by the news reporter if the Cleveland police department practiced racial profiling when he joined the department 30 years age, Kovacic replied yes. But when asked if it was still an accepted practice today he said no. When the reporter asked, how do you know? the former chief answered:

Because back then it was almost like a . . . like a policy . . . when we were in the academy there were remarks made that were . . . we had blacks that were in the academy with us, but there were remarks made that were . . . uh . . . borderline telling us to do that.

Kovacic explained that it wasn't a written policy, but they were told as part of their training to stop blacks for possible involvement in criminal activity.[22] In essence, what the chief described are the "stop and frisk" tactics, which were the antecedent to the contemporary practice of DWB, and were at the heart of the *Terry v. Ohio* case.[23]

The time period the chief was referring to would be around the late 1960s and early 1970s, the period just after the Hough Riot in 1966, which was followed in 1968 by five days of rioting in Cleveland's black Glenville neighborhood. As noted earlier, the *Terry v. Ohio* case stemmed from events involving a Cleveland police officer, the same police department that a young Kovacic would join after attending the academy roughly five to eight years later.[24] Once in the field, Kovacic and his cohort of newly trained Cleveland police officers were in all probability partnered with and trained on the job by what retired Minneapolis police chief and Bronx police force commander Anthony Bouza refers to as "wizened veterans," such as Officer Martin McFadden, who had been with the Cleveland police department 38 years at the time of his involvement in the incident that led to *Terry v. Ohio*.[25] This was a period in which the racial divisions in American society and cities such as Cleveland had hardened as Richard Nixon rode into the White House in 1968 on a campaign platform of "law and order" as he described the civil rights struggles and social unrest of the period as "the struggle of the peace forces . . . against the criminal forces."[26]

Police Training

This is the social backdrop against which Kovacic attended the police academy and this informal policy of using the race of blacks as a proxy for criminality was promoted as part of the police training that new recruits received and carried into the field. Even though the former chief's statement suggests that this informal policy of targeting blacks is no longer promoted or practiced within the department, this routine was undoubtedly bequeathed to subsequent generations of police officers as veteran officers such as those from Kovacic's era indoctrinated the rookies under their charge in the finer points of police work and imparted to them the tricks-of-the-trade in order to "make their jobs easier" and to "help them perform more efficiently and effectively on the streets." In describing the new police recruit's acculturation process into the police culture upon graduation from the academy, Bouza states, "the values are transmitted and reinforced, in an endless series of proddings, hints, examples, and nods."[27]

In studying institutions and organizational behavior, Gareth Morgan suggests that organizations are like psychic prisons in that, once the practices within an organization are ingrained into its culture and its people have become accustomed to operating in a certain manner it is difficult to change their behavior and practices. He puts forth that:

> **Organizations are psychic phenomena ultimately created and sustained by conscious and unconscious processes . . . people can actually become imprisoned or confined by the images, ideas, thoughts, and actions to which these processes give rise . . . while organizations may be socially constructed realities, these constructions are often attributed an existence and power of their own that allow them to exercise a measure of control over their creators.[28]**

Many Cleveland police officers from Kovacic's era are just now nearing the end of their careers after 30 years or more in which some likely ascended to the higher echelons of the department's command structure given their seniority in the department. Therefore, it is not unreasonable to conclude that the informal, racially based policing practices that were an institutional standard of practice prior to and during the time they joined the department as evidenced in the chief's acknowledgment and the actions of Officer McFadden in the *Terry* case, are undoubtedly still reverberating throughout the department and in turn the city of Cleveland via the informal policies, training, and customs instilled in later generations of police officers by their predecessors, in spite of current policy pronouncements against such actions.

Spatial Profiling

Evidence of these institutionalized standards of practice are apparent in the differential traffic law enforcement practices implemented by the CPD among the two different driving populations using the respective thoroughfares in this study, which is related to the concept of "spatial profiling" introduced in Chapter 3. As illustrated by the "breaks" in ticketing afforded white motorists on Chester, the police's traffic law enforcement practices or absence thereof have created a "speed free-zone" for white motorists where they can speed with relative impunity from being cited. Black motorists, on the other hand, who represent a numerical minority of the driving population on Chester, are burdened with the equivalent of a "black tax" in that they are disproportionately cited when traveling within the same public space.[29] Two sets of rules are in effect here: one for whites and one for blacks. The distinction between the two sets of law-enforcement practices being implemented along these thoroughfares in two comparable inner-city communities within the same municipal jurisdiction, governed by the same public policies, constitute "spatial profiling," which is a component of Foucault's "mechanisms of domination."[30] These mechanisms of domination are analogous to the machinery of power or control within society, of which "DWB," "spatial profiling," as well as Georges Abeyie's acts of "petit apartheid," are the nuts, bolts, and gears of the machinery.[31]

As a mechanism of domination, spatial profiling uses space and surveillance by police to produce differential outcomes for different social groups. The CPD's traffic enforcement policy objective, which suggests that "a police car with a violator pulled over demonstrates to the public that the police are visibly on patrol," and thereby has a symbolic effect on other traffic is akin to the surveillance of Foucault's carceral system, which is described as:

> **An inspecting gaze, a gaze which each individual under its weight will end by interiorising [sic] to the point that he is his own overseer, each individual thus exercising this surveillance over, and against, himself . . . a superb formula: power exercised continuously and for what turns out to be a minimal cost.[32]**

And the racial outcomes produced by the ticket distribution patterns in this study are also consistent with Foucault's characteristics of the carceral system's penality noted earlier, which "gives free rein to some," while "putting pressure on others," and "excludes some sections while making others useful."[33] These characteristics are manifest in the traffic enforcement practices employed along Chester and Kinsman as whites speed at considerably less risk of penalty on Chester than blacks, and traffic-ticket writing activities are concentrated on Kinsman to a much larger extent than on Chester. While there is ostensibly nothing inherently wrong with the department's use of such police surveillance tactics to enforce traffic laws and it would be desirable to have all citizens internalize this notion of continual observation to the point that they self-regulate their own behavior, the problem arises from the unequal use of the tactic.

Surveillance

As evidenced by the disproportionate ticketing of blacks relative to their percentage of the respective driving populations and in comparison to the ticketing of other racial groups in this study at the city, police district, and street levels, minorities, particularly blacks, are overwhelmingly the focus of this type of police surveillance. Blacks appear to have been the recipients of a heightened police scrutiny or what Foucault referred to as "subjection by illumination" regardless of the geographic context. This is most evident in the two predominately white, far Westside police districts where blacks were ticketed 233 percent and 350 percent above their 6 percent of the districts residential population, and on Chester where blacks were ticketed 64 percent above their 37 percent of the driving population.

While black motorists were the primary target of this "subjection by illumination" whites and minorities of other races were also subjected to its effect, but to a lesser extent. Whites experienced this increased visibility in the two Eastside police districts where they constituted the smallest portion of the population as well as on Kinsman where whites were also ticketed in disproportion to their percentage of the driving population. Minorities of other races encountered this subjection by illumination in all six police districts and on Chester where they too were disproportionately ticketed.[34]

As noted earlier, Cleveland is the third-most racially segregated city in the country and as reflected by the city's traffic-ticketing patterns, spatial profiling superimposes and maintains the racially segregated social order of the city. In other words, the traffic enforcement deployment patterns and practices employed by the Cleveland police department in the ticketing of each racial group in the six police districts, and in the disparity in the volume of ticketing between Chester and Kinsman reveal patterns that penalize those motorists who are "out of their place" or members of a nonnormative racial group within the context of the geographical space under surveillance or, in other words, other minority motorists in all six police districts, blacks on Chester, or whites on Kinsman.

These traffic-ticketing practices have an effect similar to that of the Slave or Black Codes during slavery, which Wintersmith suggests, were more than legislative enactments designed to govern and regulate the legal status of slaves, but were also devices to regulate the social intercourse between free whites and enslaved blacks. He states that the Black Codes were for the institutionalization of custom and practice, and the remaking of human interrelationships.[35] The spatial profiling exhibited by the traffic-enforcement patterns of the CPD can be seen as having a parallel effect by surveilling, regulating, sanctioning, and circumscribing the movement of not only blacks but members of all racial groups as they move within designated racially homogenous zones within the city.[36] The ticketing patterns in the city of Cleveland reflect the city's historic east/west, black/white racial divide and its racially segregated housing patterns which Gregory Stoup, the director of Case Western Reserve University's Center for Regional Economic Issues, compared to 1950s housing patterns in an economic analysis conducted by the center using 2000 Census data.[37]

A NOTE ABOUT RACISM

Racial profiling is an act of racism. Although *racism* is a term that is widely used, it is not very well understood. When racial behaviors are conducted by individuals either alone or in small groups, we may speak of individual racism. For example, African Americans encounter acts of individual racism in the essential areas of everyday life: in employment (applying for, keeping or being promoted in a job), shelter (trying to rent or buy housing), consumer activities (being served in stores, hotels, restaurants, etc.), transportation (driving or hailing a cab), to mention just a few. Racism significantly affects the everyday lives and life chances of African Americans.

In discussions of racism, individual racism gets most of the attention, with a clear emphasis on *intentional* acts of racism. Perhaps due to the importance of *intent* in legal proceedings, this concept is often invoked in considerations of racism. However, individual racism can be *unintentional* as well as *intentional*. A widely researched example of an action generally considered to be *unintentional* racism is when white classroom teachers have lower academic expectations of black students than they have of white students. Consequently black students tend to perform at lower levels than they would otherwise because of the unwitting activities of such teachers.

Institutional Racism

Social institutions are the social arrangements through which collective action takes place to perform functions for society. They include the family, education, business and labor, health care, housing, religion, welfare, law enforcement, and politics. These institutions operate on the basis of established formal and informal rules—policies, practices, and procedures. Policies, practices, and procedures in American institutions, established by the predominant culture, may *unintentionally* or *intentionally* be racially discriminatory. Some scholars have argued that racism in American institutions is normative, as the United States was developed on the basis of a system of racial slavery, followed by a 100-year period of legal racial discrimination. Thus, racism was embedded in the operation of the society's institutions. Even though antidiscrimination laws have been enacted, institutions may still operate the same—and be racist—unless old, established practices are changed.

While individual racism can have serious consequences, focusing on individual racism has limited usefulness because *institutional racism* is generally ignored, and it is the most serious and ingrained form of racism. Institutional racism is inherent in the operation of major institutions in this country. According to the accepted definition of institutional racism, "If racist consequences result from an institution's laws, customs, or practices, that institution is racist whether or not the individuals maintaining those practices have racist intentions."[38]

Institutional racism can be de jure or de facto and it can be intentional or unintentional. Institutional racism was given much more attention in the 1960s and the 1970s, a result of the rhetoric of the 1960s civil rights and black power movements, the Kerner Commission report,[39] and scholarly books on the subject.[40]

This is not to suggest that individual racism is not important, because it can be quite serious. The bombing of the Sixteenth Street Baptist Church in Birmingham in 1963 was a major act of individual racism. The individuals who committed this crime were not prosecuted at the time because such justice was not usually accorded to blacks in Alabama in that era. In this instance, institutional racism supported and sustained acts of individual racism.

Institutional racism is more important because its effects are widespread. While individual-level racism affects a modest number of individuals, a racist institutional policy can systematically disadvantage many members of a racial group, and the consequences can have effects over many years.

If we are going to move toward racial justice in the United States, we must define racism appropriately. The focus on intent is inappropriate, and the focus on individual acts of racism is an incomplete and misleading definition of the situation. While individual acts of racism should be addressed, more focus should be placed on institutional racism, as we hope we have demonstrated in previous chapters.

Much of current discussion about racism is aimed at individuals, calling upon them to confess to their racial biases and prejudices, as a means of solving problems of racism. These are difficult discussions because among other things they raise levels of extreme personal discomfort among the participants, while not addressing the major issues of racism. Eliminating institutional racism means eliminating the racially discriminatory practices of our institutions through changes in laws and policies.

Chapter 6 | Institutional Practices and Institutional Racism

SUMMARY AND CONCLUSION

Our study of traffic ticketing in Cleveland provides more precise methods of measuring the disproportionate ticketing of minorities within the context of a more well-defined driving population than those methods used in some studies of racial profiling. It brings the issue of institutional racism as manifested through the practices and policies of police departments into the discussion on racial profiling whereas the matter is usually approached from the individual racism perspective, that is, individual racist white police officers targeting black or other minority motorists for traffic stops. This research also helps illuminate the manner in which these policing practices help define the public space according to race, and circumscribe and regulate the movement of members of each racial group within the city, thereby reinforcing the city's racial divisions.

Moreover, this study sheds light on the manner in which the domination of space in America is racial. Racial discrimination in an institutional sense is primarily manifested spatially. This is evidenced not only by the differential administration of justice exhibited in this study but also by the historical conditions of racial segregation in housing, and education that are still salient features of American society in the 21st century. Racial profiling is to the administration of justice what "redlining" was to housing segregation, and the legal doctrine of "separate but equal" was to school segregation. It is a means by which minority citizens in general and blacks in particular are administered a different form of justice than that afforded white citizens. And its use as a law-enforcement tactic by police serves as what Websdale[41] refers to as "the lead filter of the criminal justice juggernaut" that "regulates the lives of so many among the poor, particularly black people" and provides the ever-expanding criminal justice system with "new bodies, new clientele, new cases, new sources of funding, and allegedly, new credibility."

NOTES

1. The number of other minority motorists was negligible on the predominately black roadway (Kinsman).

2. Harris compared blacks in the driving population to nonblack motorists, white and other minority motorists, in the driving population. Using this measure of nonblacks in Cleveland, they represented 60 percent of the driving population and received 42 percent of the tickets in the city, resulting in a ticketing-to-driving population ratio of 0.70 (0.42/0.60). Blacks were 40 percent of the driving population and 58 percent of those ticketed, reflecting a 1.45 ticketing-to-driving population ratio. The likelihood ratio for blacks in Cleveland in relation to nonblacks is 2.07 (1.45/0.70).

3. D. Harris, *Driving While Black: Racial Profiling on Our Nation's Highways* (New York: ACLU Department of Public Education, 1999).

4. K. Scholz (September 24, 1999). "Chief Warns Police: Issue Tickets or Else," *The Plain Dealer*, p. 21.

5. W. Wilbanks, *Myth of a Racist Criminal Justice System* (Monterey, CA: Brooks/Cole Publishing, 1987).

6. S. M. Schockley (June 16, 1999). "Another Face of Dwb: Are Southeast Clevelanders Targeted for Speed Traps?" *Cleveland Life*, p. 1.

7. Ibid.; K. Turner (August 15, 2000). "Cleveland Police Data Are Unclear on Profiling." *The Plain Dealer*, p. 4.

8. Personal communication with the president of the African American Police Supervisors Association.

9. J. M. Jones. *Prejudice and Racism* (New York: McGraw-Hill Co., 1997).

10. Ibid.

11. "Citizen Stops." Cleveland: General Police Order Cleveland Division of Police, 2002.

12. Ibid.

13. Jones, *Prejudice and Racism*.

14. Ibid, pp. 438–439.

15. Scholz, *Chief Warns Police*.

16. K. Scholz (October 2, 1999). "Police Pick Up the Pace on Tickets: Six-Week Drop in Citations Issued Ends." *The Plain Dealer*, p. 12.

17. E. Anderson *Streetwise* (Chicago: University of Chicago Press, 1990).

18. "Citizen Stops."

19. *The Mayor's Investigative Report on Racism within the Cleveland Police Department* (1999). Cleveland: Mayor's Office.

20. Ibid.; This was prior to the time the department began collecting racial demographic data on traffic tickets.

21. P. Hayes (1999). "Blacklisted: An Investigation of Racial Profiling." US: WKYC Television News.

22. Ibid.

23. "*Terry v. Ohio* Symposium Issue." (1998). *St. John's Law Review* 72: pp. 721–1546.

24. Ibid.; Hayes, *Blacklisted*, 1999.

25. K. Turner (October 26, 2003). "A Lawman's Legacy," *The Plain Dealer Sunday Magazine*, pp. 12–18; A. V. Bouza. *Police Unbound: Corruption, Abuse, and Heroism by the Boys in Blue* (Amherst, NY: Prometheus Books, 2001).

26. *Terry v. Ohio Symposium Issue.*

27. Bouza, *Police Unbound*.

28. G. Morgan. *Images of Organization* (Thousand Oaks, CA: Sage Publications, 1986).

29. Although whites were disproportionately ticketed on Kinsman, and blacks received three percentage points fewer tickets than their proportion of the driving population (90 percent – 93 percent), the same cannot be said for blacks on Kinsman in that they received 90 percent of the tickets written on this street.

30. M. Foucault. *Discipline & Punish: The Birth of the Prison* (New York: Vintage Books, 1977).

31. D. E. Georges-Abeyie (ed.). *The Criminal Justice System and Blacks* (New York: C. Boardman Co., 1984).

32. C. Gordon (ed.). *Power/Knowledge: Selected Interviews and Other Writings 1972–1977 Michel Foucault* (New York: Pantheon Books, 1980).

33. Foucault, *Discipline & Punish*.

34. As noted in Chapter 4 the small number of whites included in the violator survey on Kinsman and of other minority motorists in the driving population samples for both streets might distort the magnitude of the ticketing disparities for these groups.

35. R. F. Wintersmith. *The Police and the Black Community* (Lexington, MA: Lexington Books, 1974), p. 12.

36. Although Chester transverses several black neighborhoods on the city's predominately black Eastside, given its majority white driving population and the attendant police enforcement practices, it would be designated as a white racial zone during the business day.

37. R. L. Smith, & D. Davis (2002). "Migration Patterns Hold Back Cleveland: Segregation Takes Economic Toll, Analysts Say," *The Plain Dealer*, p. 8.

38. Jones, *Prejudice and Racism*.

39. "Report of the Commission on Civil Disorders." (1968). Washington, DC: National Advisory Commission on Civil Disorders.

40. S. Carmichael & C. Hamilton. *Black Power: The Politics of Liberation in America* (New York: Random House, 1967); L. Knowles, & K. Prewitt, (eds.), *Institutional Racism in America* (Englewood Cliffs, NJ: Prentice Hall, 1969).

41. N. Websdale. *Policing the Poor* (Boston: Northeastern University Press, 2001).

Chapter 6 | Institutional Practices and Institutional Racism

CONSEQUENCES OF RACIAL PROFILING

Traffic ticketing practices and police deployment patterns have various adverse consequences for the city and its population in general. However, blacks are most adversely impacted by these traffic enforcement practices in that the disproportionate ticketing predisposes them to increased contact with the criminal justice system, which can result in their deeper involvement with the system. Being disproportionately ticketed, particularly for young, low-income blacks, can easily create circumstances that appear overwhelming, and often have results that are less than desirable. Such was the case for Timothy Thomas, the 19-year-old African American male shot to death by a Cincinnati police officer while fleeing police after a warrant was issued for his arrest stemming from 14 tickets for minor traffic violations.[1]

While being burdened with the direct cost of fines resulting from the uneven distribution of traffic citations, blacks are also subjected to the potential indirect economic costs resulting from frequent traffic violations such as increased auto insurance rates and the loss of one's driver's license. In Ohio, motorists receive either two or four points on their driving record for each moving traffic violation not involving alcohol or resulting in a felony conviction, depending on the severity of the infraction. A person's driver's license is suspended for a minimum of one year after accumulating 12 points on his or her driving record within a two-year period. Suspension of one's driver's license can cause considerable economic hardships aside from the cost of reinstatement fees, which range from $75 for a first offense, $250 for the second offense, and $500 for each subsequent offense.[2] The loss of a driver's license would pose significant difficulties for most anyone, but its impact is extremely acute for many of the marginally employed, disproportionately black inner-city residents, and could serve to further exacerbate the already problematic jobs-to-skill set mismatch that exists in the region as many of the jobs that many inner-city residents are most qualified for are located outside of the central city.

COSTS OF RACIAL PROFILING

Some investigators cite the costs of racial profiling, costs to individuals, communities, and the public. Harris[3] points to the situations of professional black men being stopped for no apparent reason, other than their race. He tells three stories that typify how racial profiling harasses innocent black men. One is the case of a black vice-president of a large bank in Toledo, Ohio, who is also president of the Toledo school board. This man, dressed in his banker's suit, was stopped because his car "did not have a front license plate." The police officer asked him if he had a gun or drugs. When the man indicated he did not, the officer forced him to stand with his hands against the patrol car while the officer patted him down, saying that he was making sure he did not have a gun. The man was further embarrassed to see colleagues with whom he had been meeting earlier that day driving by, witnessing the event, and wondering what he had done to be in police custody. Although the man did not receive a ticket, a citation, or a warning, he was embarrassed and frustrated at the treatment he received. This is an example of the emotional distress that many innocent African American men experience. In this man's mind, a white man in business suit, tie, and topcoat in a late-model upscale automobile would not have been ordered from the car, frisked, and asked if he had weapons or drugs.

A second story told by Harris concerns a black man who headed a large government agency, who drove to a high school gymnasium in a predominantly white neighborhood to work out. As he pulled up and parked his car, a police car came "screeching up behind me [with] the lights flashing," blocking him so that he could not drive away. Upon seeing the man's official government identification, the officer immediately went back to his car and drove off, without saying anything or otherwise apologizing.

Another black male, who lived in an upscale, predominantly white neighborhood was continually followed by a police car when he jogged near his home. This continued even after he responded to the police officer's query about what he was doing there by indicating that he lived in the neighborhood. After this type of surveillance continued, he quit jogging and eventually moved his family from the area.

This kind of continuing treatment is not without effect, as there are psycho-emotional costs. Some investigators suggest that the consequences of exposure to racism should be viewed as psychological trauma for minorities.[4] At the level of severe stress it might be post-traumatic stress disorder (PTSD). For example, the DSM-IV diagnostic criteria for PTSD[5] include the following:

1. An individual experienced, witnessed, or confronted events that involved actual or threatened death or serious injury or threat to physical integrity of self or others, and
2. His response involved intense helplessness, fear, or horror.

Responses of some victims of racial profiling harassment are similar to clinical PTSD victims. For instance, many African American men tend to be hyper-vigilant, ascertaining whether their situation or surroundings are "safe" for a black man.

INCARCERATION TRENDS

One of the results of racial profiling is the growing disparity in incarceration of African Americans and Hispanics. More than 60 percent of people in prison are now racial and ethnic minorities. For black males in their twenties, 1 in every 8 is in prison or jail on any given day. These trends have been accelerated by the disproportionate impact of the "war on drugs." One of every three black males born today can expect to go to prison if the current trends continue.[6]

In the latter quarter of the twentieth century the United States saw a significant increase in the number of its citizens incarcerated in prisons and jails. It is now the world's leader in incarceration. By 2006 the rate of incarceration had increased to 751 inmates per 100,000 persons in the population, which was well ahead of the second place Russia, where the rate was 628 per 100,000 persons. Between 1880 and 1975, the state and federal prison population grew at a fairly consistent and negligible rate, reflecting little more than the growth in the general population. However, a real growth spurt occurred after 1970 (see Figure 1). The number of inmates in state and federal prisons increased more than seven-fold, from less than 200,000 in 1970 to 1,570,861 by the end of 2006. An additional 766,010 were in local jails, raising the total number in prisons and jails to more than 2.2 million.[7]

As Figure 7.1 shows, African Americans were a large segment of this rapid increase in prisoners. One in nine (11.7 percent) black males age 25–29 was in prison or jail in 2006, compared to one in 59 (1.7 percent) white males; 40 percent of persons in prison or jail in 2006 were black.

In 1903, W. E. DuBois proposed that the problem of the 20th century was the color line. This prediction was exemplified in the criminal justice system as race was a continuing issue in criminal justice processing throughout the century. For example, in 1910, African Americans were 11 percent of the population in the United States but 31 percent of the prison population. They accounted for 405 of the 455 executions for rape between 1930 and 1972. Sentencing laws were overtly discriminatory, with the harshest sanctions given to blacks who victimized whites.[8]

The convict leasing system was a southern phenomenon, filling prisons with black men who were used as cheap labor by local industries. However, as African Americans began to migrate to northern cities in the early twentieth century, the proportion of blacks in all prisons began to increase. In 1926, African Americans were 21 percent of all new admissions into America's prisons. By 1964 they were one-third of all new prisoners. By the 1990s they were more than half of the admissions.[9]

For two-thirds of the century, segregation and discrimination were legally practiced, and the criminal justice system was often a major contributor to the problem. Criminal justice practices were key instruments of segregation and discrimination. In the second half of the century, laws and U.S. Supreme Court rulings made racial discrimination unconstitutional. The assumption was that discrimination would be diminished. Overt discrimination in law enforcement and the courts have been diminished. However, current criminal justice practices suggest that racial discrimination is still operative, as serious racial disparities have persisted into the twenty-first century.

African Americans have continued to have a significantly greater lifetime likelihood of going to a state or federal prison than white Americans. In 1974 black males were over six times more likely than white males; in 1991 black males were 6.7 times more likely than white males; and in 2001 they were 5.5 times as likely.[10]

FIGURE 7.1 Black and White Prison Admissions, Historical

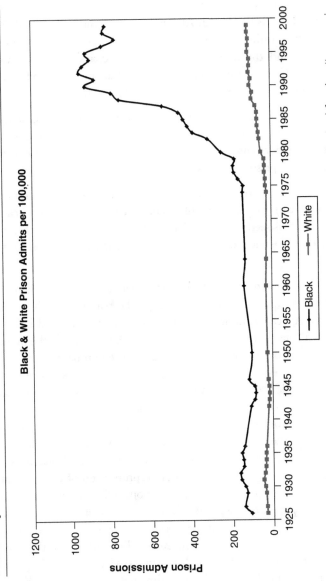

Black & White Prison Admits per 100,000

Prison Admissions

1200 1000 800 600 400 200 0

1925 1930 1935 1940 1945 1950 1955 1960 1965 1970 1975 1980 1985 1990 1995 2000

Black — White

Pamela Oliver. 2007, *Racial Disparities in Criminal Justice*. The Wisconsin Racial Disparities Project. Retrieved from http://www.ssc.wisc.edu/~oliver/RACIAL/RacialDisparities.htm

105

DRUGS AND CRIMINAL JUSTICE

The American correctional population is increasingly African American. This racial disparity has several ominous manifestations:

- Nationally, African American males are incarcerated at 8.2 times the incarceration rate of whites.[11]
- On any given day one-third of all African American males in the 20–29 age group are in the criminal justice system (i.e., in prison or jail) or on probation or parole, and the rate is higher in many cities[12]: For example, in Washington, DC, the rate is 42 percent; in Baltimore, Maryland, it is 56 percent; and in Jacksonville, Florida, it is 75 percent.[13]

Illegal drugs play a major role in the increase in imprisonment. One in four jail inmates in 2002 was in jail for a drug offense, compared to one in ten in 1983; drug offenders constituted 20 percent of state prison inmates and 55 percent of federal prison inmates in 2001.[14]

Major reasons for the increasing racial disparity in prison incarceration are illegal drugs and drug prosecution policy and practices. Black Americans are prosecuted and imprisoned for drug offenses at a much higher rate than white Americans, and imprisoned at a rate far beyond their participation in illegal drug activities.

It is generally well known that more African Americans are arrested and prosecuted for crack cocaine than whites. Perhaps the reason there is not more outcry from the African American community is the widely held belief that crack cocaine is a "black urban drug," that African Americans are the predominant users of crack cocaine while whites are the predominant users of powder cocaine. Two perceptions feed this idea: One is that crack, since it is less expensive than powder cocaine, is much more accessible to inner-city blacks; the other is that most of the criminal activity—and criminal justice activity—concerning crack involves African Americans. Contrary to popular opinion, however, whites are the predominant users of crack, as well as powder cocaine, heroin, marijuana, and other illegal drugs. In fact, whites and blacks use illegal drugs commensurate with their respective proportion of the population. Whites are 75 percent of the American population; and they are approximately 75 percent of all illegal drug users. Blacks are 12.3 percent of the population and they are approximately the same proportion (14 percent) of all illegal drug users. However, black drug offenders are treated differentially in the criminal justice system. They are 34 percent of drug arrests, 53 percent of drug convictions, and 63 percent of all drug offenders admitted to state prisons.[15]

As shown in Chapter 4, one of the places where the excess arrests of African Americans occur is in traffic stops and searches. This disparate treatment at the hands of the criminal justice system is adversely affecting not just African Americans in general and African American males in particular; it is wreaking havoc on families and communities. The correctional system is itself in dire need of correction.

No argument is being made here to condone criminal behavior. In fact, the removal of serious offenders from a community has definite benefits. However, doing so—in the present environment of disproportionately imprisoning these high numbers of nonviolent offenders—may be producing unintended consequences that outweigh the desired correctional objectives. What is currently happening on a broad scale is the removal of large numbers of young African American males from communities, harming the ability of those communities to form the human capital necessary to sustain and perpetuate themselves. The large-scale incarcerations occurring in many cities remove potential wage-earners, disrupt family relationships, and increase a community's sense of alienation from the larger society.[16] Consequently, some steps toward resolution of this problem are urgently needed.

FELONY DISENFRANCHISEMENT

Felony disenfranchisement is an obstacle to participation in democratic life which is exacerbated by racial disparities in the criminal justice system. In most states felony conviction results in the loss of the right to vote either temporarily (during incarceration) or permanently. Forty-six states deny felons the right to vote during the time they are incarcerated. Thirty-one states deny the vote for prisoners and those on probation or parole; and 13 states take away the right to vote for life.[17]

Nationwide, more than 5.3 million Americans who have been convicted of a felony are denied access to the one fundamental right that is the foundation of all other rights, the right to vote. Over 2 million, or 38 percent, of these disfranchised individuals are African Americans.[18] A report by the Legal Defense Fund details that a staggering 13 percent of all African American men in this country—and in some states up to one-third of the entire African American male population—are denied the right to vote. Given current rates of incarceration, an astonishing one in three of the next generation of black men will be disfranchised at some point during their lifetime.[19]

COLLATERAL CONSEQUENCES

The high rates of incarceration have effects far beyond the individual offender. They are having devastating consequences for families, communities, and the nation.[20] Hagan and Dinovitzer summarizes this point as follows:

> **The Collateral costs of imprisonment may be extensive. The most obvious concern is that the effects of imprisonment damage the human and social capital of those who are incarcerated, their families, and their communities . . . Imprisonment may engender negative consequences for <u>offenders</u> whose employment prospects after release are diminished; for <u>families</u> who suffer losses both emotional and financial; for <u>children</u> who suffer emotional and behavioral problems due to the loss of a parent, financial strain, and possible displacement into the care of others; for <u>communities</u> whose stability is threatened due to the loss of working males; and for <u>other social institutions</u> that are affected by the budgetary constraints imposed by the increase in spending on incarceration.[21]**

Employment

Perhaps even more problematic than losing the right to vote is losing much of the ability to gain employment. Incarceration hurts the economic stability of black communities by reducing the workforce. This is done in two ways. First, the workforce is depleted with so many black men in the criminal justice system and out of the labor force. Second, felony records reduce the ability of black men to find employment.[22]

Family

Families in black communities are affected in at least two ways by incarceration. The majority of prison inmates tend to be parents. About 2 percent of the nation's children had a parent in prison in 1999, with about half of them living with their children before incarceration.[23] Because of the disparity in incarceration, black children are the most likely to have an incarcerated parent. As such they are deprived of the support of the missing parent. Seven percent of black children had a parent in prison in 1999. Children of incarcerated parents, predominantly a black issue, experience various psycho-emotional issues, including depression, anxiety, and problems in school. One study, reported by Roberts[24] found that some children of incarcerated mothers experienced trauma from the separation that resembled posttraumatic stress disorder.

Another way that incarceration hurts families is by the higher levels of unemployment that ex-convicts face. An increasing proportion of African American men are not working. A part of the reason is the economic restructuring that occurred in the 1960s and 1970s which saw manufacturing jobs move away from urban areas where the majority of blacks lived.[25] From 1960 to 2009, the proportion of African American men not working (either unemployed or not in the labor force) grew from just over 30 percent to almost 50 percent. Without jobs, such men were not considered a part of the "marriageable-mate pool,"[26] a factor in the rise in female-headed households.[27]

The growing proportion of African American men with felony records has a negative effect on employment of these men and therefore on marriage. The situation is currently in a crisis, as over 70 percent of all babies born to black women are born to lone mothers, women who are not married. This situation presents many disadvantages for these children, as 80 percent of all lone mother families are in poverty. Poverty is more than an inconvenience, it adversely affects the life chances of children. In Table 7.1 shows several problems that poverty creates for children. For example, poor children in comparison to nonpoor children are nearly twice as likely to be in poor or fair health (1.8), 3.5 times more likely to have lead poisoning, and 70 percent (1.7) more likely to die as an infant.

TABLE 7.1 Selected Population-Based Indicators of Well-Being for Poor and Nonpoor Children in the United States

Indicator	Percentage of Poor Children (unless noted)	Percentage of Nonpoor children (unless noted)	Ratio of Poor to Nonpoor Children
Physical Health Outcomes			
• Reported to be in fair to poor health	11.7	6.5	1.8
• Low birth weight (less than 2,500 grams)	1.0	0.6	1.7
• Lead poisoning (blood lead levels 10 µ/dl or greater)	16.3	4.7	3.5
• Infant mortality	1.4 deaths/ 100 live births	0.8 deaths/ 100 live births	1.7
• Deaths during childhood (0 to 14 years)	1.2	0.8	1.5
• Stunted growth	10.0	5.0	2.0
• Number of days spent in bed in past year	5.3 days	3.8 days	2.0

(continued)

TABLE 7.1 (*Continued*)

Indicator	Percentage of Poor Children (unless noted)	Percentage of Nonpoor children (unless noted)	Ratio of Poor to Nonpoor Children
• Number of short-stay hospital episodes in past year per 1,000 children	81.3 stays	41.2 stays	2.0
Cognitive Outcomes			
• Developmental delay and long-term developmental deficits	5.0	3.8	1.3
• Learning disability	8.3	6.1	1.4
School Achievement Outcomes			
• Grade Repetition	28.8	14.1	2.0
• Ever expelled or suspended	11.9	6.1	2.0
• High school dropout	21.0	9.6	2.2
Emotional or Behavioral Outcomes			
• Parent reports child has ever had an emotional or behavioral problem that lasted three months or more	16.4	12.7	1.3
Other			
• Female teens who had an out-of-wedlock birth	11.0	3.6	3.1
• Economically inactive at age 24	15.9	8.3	1.9
• Experienced hunger (food insufficiency) at least once in past year	15.9	1.6	9.9
• Reported cases of child abuse and neglect	5.4	0.8	6.8
• Violent crimes (experienced by family)	5.4	2.6	2.1
• Afraid to go out (percentage of family heads who report they are afraid to go out in their neighborhoods.)	19.5	8.7	2.2

Source: J. Brooks-Gunn and G. J. Duncan. "The Effects of Poverty on Children. The Future of Children," *Children and Poverty*. Vol. 7, No. 2 – Summer/Fall 1997.

Poor children are also more likely to have developmental delays and learning disabilities. They are more than twice as likely to be a high school dropout. And poor female teens are more than three times as likely to have an out-of-wedlock birth. While some single mother families, approximately 20 percent, will be able to avoid these issues by avoiding poverty, approximately 80 percent will not.

POLICY RECOMMENDATIONS

First, city and law enforcement officials must have the political will and fortitude to address this most sensitive and perplexing issue of racial profiling. They cannot afford to continue to deny the existence of a problem, particularly without first collecting the requisite data and thoroughly investigating the matter. And although the police department in Cleveland began voluntarily collecting racial data on tickets, city officials here and in jurisdictions where legislation does not exist, should pass policies prohibiting the use of racial profiling and requiring the collection of racial demographic data on every traffic stop, not just those resulting in tickets. Passing such legislation will help establish uniform data collection procedures and standards and provide oversight and the necessary financial resources to effectively carry out this initiative. Enactment of municipal legislation will also help establish sanctions for noncompliance with the legislation.

Law enforcement officials should work with political and community leaders to address the issue of police deployment patterns that produce racially biased effects. A means of providing each community with the appropriate police protection and services without residents having to sacrifice their civil rights needs to be developed. As evidenced by the confluence of the present traffic enforcement deployment patterns and the existing implicit traffic-ticketing quota, reduced police discretion diminishes the significance of race in the distribution of tickets. Therefore, efforts should be made to reduce the level of subjectivity of the individual police officer in traffic law enforcement. This can be accomplished through the use of technology, namely by equipping police cruisers with video cameras and installing cameras at stoplights on the busiest thoroughfares or those with the highest incidences of speeding and traffic light violations. This will not only ward against racially biased traffic enforcement it will also protect police against questionable charges of racial profiling or abuse by providing an objective record of events.

Law enforcement officials should not approach these efforts defensively but rather as an opportunity to address an issue that negatively affects at least 40 percent of this city's driving population and over half of its residents and can only serve to improve relations between the police and the African American community. Nor should police officials view this as an attack on police as "racist." What is at issue here are institutionalized practices that are embodied in the informal policies that have been unwittingly passed on to the current generation of law enforcement officers and are manifest in racially discriminatory outcomes. Although no one individual is responsible for creating these circumstances those administrators at the top of the institutions and organizations from which these racially biased outcomes emanate must take the lead in rectifying them. And not only will the black community benefit from these efforts—in Cleveland and elsewhere—but the cities and regions overall will benefit both economically and socially.

NOTES

1. L. Barandes, T. Loftus, P. Segner, & J. Sweeney (2004). "A Pattern of Suspicion: Dateline Investigates Claims of Racial Profiling." US: MSNBC.com.

2. "Ohio Revised Code Title XLV Motor Vehicles, Aeronautics, Watercraft, Driver's License Suspension, Cancellation, Revocation." In *Chapter 4510, Sec. 0.3.07.*

3. D. Harris. *Profiles in Injustice: Why Racial Profiling Cannot Work* (New York: The New Press, 2002).

4. J. Sanchez-Hucles (June 2, 1999). "Racism: Emotional; Abusiveness and Psychological Trauma for Ethnic Minorities," *Journal of Emotional Abuse,* issue 2: pp. 69–87.

5. American Psychiatric Association. *Diagnostic and Statistical Manual of Mental Disorders*, 4th ed. (Washington, DC: APA, 1994).

6. The Sentencing Project (2010). "Racial Disparity." Available at http://www .sentencingproject.org/template/page.cfm?id=122

7. The Sentencing Project (2007). "Facts About Prisons and Prisoners." Available at www.sentencingproject.org.

8. K. Rosich. *Race, Ethnicity, and the Criminal Justice System* (Washington, DC: American Sociological Association, 2007). Available at http://asanet.org.

9. J. G. Miller. *Search and Destroy: African-American Males in the Criminal Justice System* (New York: Cambridge University Press, 1996); Human Rights Watch (May 2000). *Punishment and Prejudice: Racial Disparities in the War on Drugs.* Available at http://www.hrw.org/reports/2000/usa/

10. T. P. Bonczar. *Prevalence of Imprisonment in the U.S. Population. 1974–2001* (Washington, DC: Bureau of Justice Statistics, 2003).

11. Rosich, *Race, Ethnicity, and the Criminal Justice System.*

12. M. Mauer, & T. Huling, *Intended and Unintended Consequences: State Racial Disparities in Imprisonment* (Washington, DC: The Sentencing Project, 1995).

13. J. G. Miller. *Search and Destroy: African-American Males in the Criminal Justice System* (New York: Cambridge University Press, 1996).

14. The Sentencing Project, *Crack Cocaine Sentencing Policy: Unjustified and Unreasonable* (Washington, DC: The Sentencing Project, 1997).

15. Human Rights Watch (April 2003). *Incarcerated America.* Available at http:// hrw.org/backgrounder/usa/incarceration/.

16. M. Mauer. *Intended and Unintended Consequences: State Racial Disparities in Imprisonment* (Washington, DC: The Sentencing Project, 1997).

17. D. E. Roberts (2001). *Criminal Justice and Black Families: The Collateral Damage of Over-Enforcement.* U.C. Davis L. Rev. 1005.

18. The Sentencing Project, 2010.

19. Legal Defense Fund (2010). *Free the Vote: Unlocking Democracy in the Cells and on the Streets.* Available at http://naacpldf.org/files/publications/Free%20the%20 Vote.pdf.

20. Roberts, *Criminal Justice and Black Families.*

21. J. Hagan, & R. Dinovitzer (1999). Collateral Consequences of Imprisonment for Children, Communities, and Prisoners. *Crime and Justice,* volume 26, "Prisons," p. 122.

22. D. Pager (March 2003). "The Mark of a Criminal Record," *American Journal of Sociology 108* (5): 937–975.

23. Roberts, *Criminal Justice and Black Families.*

24. Ibid.

25. W. J. Wilson. *The Truly Disadvantaged: The Inner City, the Underclass, and Public Policy* (Chicago: University of Chicago Press, 1987); W. J. Wilson, *When Work Disappears: The World of the New Urban Poor.* New York: Knopf, 1996).

26. Wilson, *The Truly Disadvantaged.*

27. M. B. Tucker, & C. Mitchell-Kernan. *The Decline in Marriage Among African Americans* (New York: Russell Sage Foundation, 1995).

8

EPILOGUE:
A JOURNEY FROM
RESEARCH STUDY
TO PUBLIC POLICY

*(In this chapter Ronnie Dunn provides a personal account of the chain of reactions
and the impact on policy after he provided a copy of the study to city officials.)*[1]

RACE AND POLITICS: CLEVELAND STYLE

As noted earlier, the city of Cleveland is historically significant in regard to
race and politics in that it was the first major American city to elect an African
American mayor with the election of Carl B. Stokes in 1967. At the time,
Cleveland and its African American community, which made up only 37 percent
of the city's population, were arguably the most progressive city and black
community in the country. As Persons points out, the election of the more

than 300 black mayors in cities throughout the country since Stokes's election is the most salient symbol of black empowerment.[2] Cleveland has the largest African American population in the state of Ohio, and Cuyahoga County, which is the Democratic Party stronghold in the state. And this Democratic stronghold and its significant black voting bloc were instrumental in delivering the state of Ohio to Barack Obama, making him the first African American president of the United States.

Despite Cleveland's historic first and vital role in racial politics, today the city is racially polarized along a black/white racial faultline and is regularly listed as one of the most racially segregated cities in the country. This racial polarization is clearly manifested in the city's politics. While several black Clevelanders had held elected office at both the local and state level during the late 19th and earlier 20th century, it wasn't until the election of Stokes that blacks acquired political positions and power in Cleveland that was not the result of their political allegiance to the political machine, and powerful, white, elite politicians and businessmen.[3]

In an effort to consolidate the political power and influence of blacks within the Democratic Party, Stokes and his supporters formed the 21st District Democratic Caucus. The party denied Stokes and his followers' demands for say in the selection of candidates running for office and as a result, the Caucus left the party and organized what in essence constituted a third party. Operating as a nonpartisan political organization, the Caucus provided the infrastructure to direct the black vote in a manner to facilitate the continued black leadership to the mayor's office, and to give the Caucus a decisive voice in the election of representatives at the local, state, and federal levels of government.[4] The Caucus was successful in increasing black political representation at all levels of government and in redistricting the boundaries of the 21st Congressional District (now the 11th) to consolidate the black voting bloc on the racially segregated Eastside of the city and county. This ensured black representation in the District with Stokes's older brother Louis being elected and holding the congressional seat for 30 years (1966–1996), followed by the late Stephanie Tubbs-Jones who held the seat 12 years before her unexpected death from an aneurysm in 2008. The congressional seat is currently held by Tubbs-Jones's former chief-of-staff, Marcia L. Fudge.

Although the 21st District Caucus's objective was to institutionalize the political power of the black community, its influence was soon diminished with Stokes's decision to not seek reelection for a third term, the defeat of his chosen successor by white-ethnic Democrat Ralph Perk in 1971, and internal strife between the Caucus's three leaders including the mayor's brother, Congressman Stokes. This further eroded the Caucus's cohesive effect over the black vote, thus leading to the demise of the political clout that the black community exercised through the Caucus. With two of the Caucuses' leaders abandoning the Caucus, black elected officials migrated back to the Cuyahoga Democratic Party in droves.[5]

Since Stokes's election in 1967 there has been an informal policy at City Hall that if the mayor is black the president of City Council will be white and vice versa. Although this racial compromise has been challenged at times within City Hall, it has held true since 1967. The city has had three African American mayors including the current mayor, who is in his second four-year term and served as City Council president prior to being elected mayor. In addition to having elected three black mayors, blacks have held a significant number of seats on the City Council for some time. At the time of Stokes's election blacks held one-third of the seats on City Council (11 of 33). The size of City Council was reduced from 33 to 21 councilpersons due to the precipitous loss of population in the city during the 70s and 80s. Until this year, 10 blacks and one Hispanic member of Council constituted a majority of the 21 seat legislative body. A referendum was passed in 2009 that further downsized Council in light of further population decline. Blacks currently hold 9 (47 %) of the 19 council seats while the one Hispanic councilmember lost his seat.[6]

In spite of the significant presence of blacks at the highest levels of city government and throughout City Hall, some black elected officials in the city demonstrate a seeming reluctance to address potentially contentious issues related to race such as racial profiling. The attitudes and actions of these officials regarding race-related issues reflects what Rice refers to as "passive representation."[7] This is when members of underrepresented groups within traditionally white-dominated institutions or organizations such as government or law enforcement agencies provide a numerical presence of the groups they are assumed to represent yet do not seek to change the organizational culture of the institution or affect the manner in which the organization interacts with members of the underrepresented cultural groups both internally and externally.

Even armed with compelling empirical evidence such as that included in this study that documented the disproportionate adverse effects that certain practices have on their constituency in this hyper-segregated, black majority city, some black elected representatives were apathetic about taking on such issues. There were some black elected officials on the other hand, who exhibited "active representation"[8] as illustrated by their willingness to address the racial disparities in traffic ticketing and law enforcement practices that this research showed disproportionately affected blacks, and to a lesser degree other minorities in the city. A report of this research was first offered to an African American city councilman who was a personal friend of the first author and who served on Council's Public Safety Committee at the time. It was anticipated that he would welcome the opportunity to take the study and present it to his colleagues on Council and be the beneficiary of the political capital that would accrue from crafting legislation to address the racial disparities identified in the study. This, however, was not the case. The councilman nervously declined the offer and hastily suggested the study be given to the chair of the Public Safety Committee, a less-tenured, but ambitious African American member of Council who held aspirations of running for mayor.

Accordingly, a hard copy of the study was delivered to the office of the chair of the Public Safety Committee. Upon receiving the report and being given a summary of its major findings, this councilman immediately placed a telephone call to a columnist for the city's major daily newspaper, *The Plain Dealer*. The reporter also requested and received a copy of the study. After the reporter reviewed the study and conducted a telephone interview regarding the study's research methods and major findings, a column entitled "Tale of Two Roads Reveals Racial Divide" appeared in the newspaper.[9] This article primarily focused on the street-level analysis comparing the disparity in traffic ticketing on the two major thoroughfares, Kinsman and Chester.

After this article appeared in the newspaper, the local news affiliate of the Fox Television network contacted Cleveland State University's public affairs office requesting an interview regarding the study. I was contacted while traveling over the Fourth of July weekend and agreed to conduct the television interview upon my return. After the initial article appeared in the newspaper, the mayor's office also contacted the university requesting a copy of the study while I was still out of state.

After returning to Cleveland, I mailed a copy of the study to the mayor's office, copies of which were also provided to the city's safety director and chief of police. The next morning I also met with a news crew from the television station on Chester Avenue, the major traffic artery in the study primarily used by white motorists commuting to the downtown area. The news report focused on the street-level analysis and disparities in ticketing. It also included man-on-the-street interviews with African Americans who concurred with the study's findings that police disproportionately targeted black motorists by concentrating their ticketing activities along Kinsman Road. The news report concluded with the reporter saying that the city safety director was reviewing the study and while he had some questions regarding the manner in which the numbers were compiled, they would take the study seriously. The report aired on the station during its 6:00 and 10:00 p.m. news broadcasts and again during its noon broadcast the following day.

I soon received another call from the newspaper columnist who wrote the initial article and she informed me that she had received over 300 emails and telephone calls regarding the column, the most overwhelming response she had received to any column up to that time. She wanted to write a follow-up column and have me respond to some of the questions and issues raised by readers, which I did. The interview lasted approximately 45 minutes and addressed all of the relevant questions and issues raised by her readers. The second column titled "Tickets for One and All"[10] appeared in the paper on July 9. I was also contacted and interviewed by reporters from the Columbus and Cleveland offices of the *Call & Post*, the oldest weekly black newspaper in the state of Ohio and articles appeared in editions of the paper in both cities.

In addition, I was a guest on several talk-radio shows during this time. While the hosts of all of these radio shows were African Americans, they seemed to have a somewhat racially mixed listening audience based on the persons who called the station with questions or comments. In general, the public response to the study and its findings appeared to be split between the races, with blacks supporting its findings and whites questioning its findings. Many of the questions raised by the callers were similar to those of the readers of the newspaper column which I addressed in the second article and that had already been accounted for in the study.

I was soon contacted by the city safety director's office to meet with him to discuss the study. The meeting was scheduled for early August, a little over a month after the first news article on the research had appeared in the local media. The day before the scheduled meeting with the safety director, I received a call from an African American councilwoman who informed me that a high-ranking African American official within the police department wanted to meet with me before my meeting the next day. I called this official and we met in their home that night to discuss the study. They informed me that they also initially did not accept the findings of the study as they had heard them reported in the news media, and as they stated, neither did most officers in the department, including black officers. But after actually reading the study, this individual concluded that the study and its findings were valid and after discussing the study with other blacks in the department and convincing them to look at it objectively, they too concurred that the major arguments raised in the study were accurate. This individual cautioned me that the mayor's administration had met with a "white researcher" from another university in the state in an effort to find someone to conduct a study that would refute the study's findings. Needless to say, this information created some apprehension regarding the meeting with the safety director the next day.

As I sat in the outer office waiting to meet with the safety director I didn't know quite what to expect given this new information from the night before. The safety director, an African American male in roughly the same age range as myself (early 40s) emerged from his office door and welcomed me into his office. After our initial greeting and a brief discussion of our backgrounds, much to my surprise, he began the conversation regarding the study by thank-ing me. He thanked me because he had only been in the safety director posi-tion for six months, having previously served as the city prosecutor, and as he reported, while he knew "there were problems (within the police department) this gave him something to hang his hat on." He told me how he had read the study over the weekend, sitting in the park under a tree while visiting with his end-laws in Columbus. And he said that as an African American male having grown up in the greater Cleveland area, the study resonated with him.

We discussed the recommendations made in the study, which the safety direc-tor said the city was considering and further exploring in order to determine the feasibility of implementing them and their potential effectiveness. He specifically stated that the city would immediately address the issues related to the deployment of traffic-enforcement patrols along the major thorough-fares identified in the study. He also stated that the police department had applied for a federal grant to implement a small pilot program to fund the use of video cameras in police cruisers, and that the city was looking at other cities where traffic cameras were in use.

THE STUDY'S INFLUENCE ON PUBLIC POLICY

This study has had a considerable impact on public policy, both in the city of Cleveland and in other jurisdictions throughout the state of Ohio. The most immediate action the city of Cleveland took to address some of the dispari-ties in traffic ticketing identified in the study was to revise the deployment patterns of traffic-enforcement units. Although the revised deployment plans were not publicized by the police department, the safety director reported such actions were taken (personal communication). In addition, in subsequent discussions of the research, motorists who utilized this thoroughfare during their commute reported increased traffic-enforcement patrols along Chester Avenue.[11] I also observed increased traffic stops on this thoroughfare after the study's release. The city also raised the speed limit on 34 streets in the city from 25 to 35 mph; 21 on the predominately black East Side of the city and 13 on the West Side, which is predominately white. Public officials' think-ing on this measure was obviously that by increasing the speed limit on these thoroughfares the likelihood of motorists being ticketed for speeding would be reduced. Kinsman Road was one of the streets on the East Side where the speed limit was adjusted. It was set at 35 mph consistently except for school zones, thus eliminating the six variations in the speed limit along the road's less than 5-mile span as identified in the study, which had created what were referred to as "speed traps" by motorists traveling this route.

Traffic Cameras

The most significant impact from the recommendations of the study was that the city installed 42 traffic cameras throughout the city. In November 2005 the city installed the first six of 36 stationary traffic cameras that would eventually be installed along traffic arteries throughout the city. The automated cameras were placed at designated intersections to catch those motorists who ran the red light or who exceeded the speed limit. There are also six mobile traffic cameras in police cruisers that patrol the city's streets.

The cameras capture the image of violators' vehicles and front and rear license plates as it triggers a mechanism embedded in the street in the intersections after either running the red light or exceeding the posted speed limit. The fine for being caught running a red light by one of the traffic light cameras is $100, while the fine for being caught speeding by one of the cameras can range from $100 to $200 depending on the rate of speed above the posted speed limit.

The traffic camera tickets are administered by the traffic unit in the Clerk of Courts Office where the images are transmitted to computer and the actual ticket is generated. Each traffic ticket is then reviewed by two Cleveland police officers who determine the validity of the infraction by considering the road and weather conditions and any other potentially extenuating circumstances. Once the validity of each ticket is established the ticket is then sent to the address of the individual to whom the vehicle's license plate is registered (personal interview with the clerk of courts and tour of automated traffic-ticketing unit, 2006).

The city activated the first six cameras in November 2005. A total of 2,380 traffic tickets were administered by the traffic cameras within their first month of operation (November 29 through December 29, 2005). Of the total number of tickets administered during this one-month period 2,309 (97%) were administered on Chester Avenue, the major thoroughfare utilized by a primarily white driving population commuting to and from the downtown area as noted in this study. These 2,309 tickets generated from the traffic cameras located at 71st and Chester over this one-month period are more than the total 1,682 tickets written along the length of Chester during the two-year observation period (April 1999 to May 2001) covered in the study. In comparison, 6,366 traffic tickets were written on Kinsman Avenue during the two years of the study. This constitutes a 3.8-to-1 ratio between the number of tickets administered on Kinsman and the number of citations written on Chester during the same period. The total number of traffic camera tickets disseminated on Chester during just one month represents a 37 percent increase over the two-year total in this study.

During the course of the 24-month study observation period an average of 70 tickets per month were written on Chester. This constitutes a 2,239 difference between the number of tickets administered by traffic cameras on Chester in one month in comparison to the monthly average during this two-year period. Using the $100 minimum amount of each of the traffic camera citations the under-enforcement of traffic laws along Chester over the course of the two-year study period could have cost the city as much as $223,900 per month or $5,373,600 (if the monthly average number of traffic violations remained constant).

While the race of the motorists is not noted on the traffic camera tickets and thus the race of the motorists ticketed during this one-month period is not readily known, the *Plain Dealer* reported that 11 percent (254) of the traffic camera citations on Chester were administered to residents of Cleveland Heights and Shaker Heights.[12] These two inner-ring suburbs on Cleveland's East Side have populations that are 52.5 percent white, 41.8 percent black, and 5.7 percent other races and 59.9 percent white, 34.1 percent black, and 6 percent other minorities respectively. Cleveland Heights' driving age population is 58 percent white and 42 percent black while Shaker Heights' driving age population is 60 percent white and 40 percent black.[13] In this study's street-level analysis of traffic ticket data, blacks were 37.2 percent of the driving population on Chester (during rush hour) and received 61 percent of the tickets, while whites were 60.5 percent of the driving population and received 34 percent of the tickets, and other minorities were 2.4 percent of the motorists on Chester and received 5 percent of the tickets written there. Although it is not possible to precisely determine the racial distribution of those motorists from Cleveland Heights and Shaker Heights that were ticketed by the traffic camera on Chester during this one-month period, all else being equal, it is highly likely that the racial disparities in ticketing distribution in this sample was not as great as that found in this study, and it more accurately reflects the proportion of the driving population that each racial group represents.

The preliminary evidence from the first month of traffic tickets administered using the traffic cameras support the contention that the Cleveland Police Department's traffic-enforcement activities and deployment patterns were concentrated on those thoroughfares primarily utilized by black motorists such as Kinsman, while there was relatively little enforcement of the traffic laws on those thoroughfares primarily used by white and suburban motorists commuting to the downtown area of which Chester Avenue is representative.

And while the traffic cameras provide an objective record of traffic violators regardless of their race, ethnicity, religion, gender, economic class, or any other social identifier or stratifier and have been credited with enhancing safety and reducing traffic violations at the sites where cameras are located, one of the unintended consequences of the recommendation has been the revenue stream generated from the traffic cameras' use. Public officials' estimates of the annual revenue generated from the cameras have ranged from as low as $6 million to as high as $12 million. During the 12-month period between February 2008 and February 2009 the traffic cameras generated at least $10.8 million in revenue, approximately $6.19 million of which went to the city and the remainder of which went to the company that operates the traffic cameras.[14] To date, the traffic cameras have generated a reported $24 million in revenue since 2006.[15]

Moreover, the recommendations from the study have had statewide implications. At the state level the use of traffic cameras was adopted by other municipalities throughout Ohio including the cities of East Cleveland, Garfield Heights, Akron, and Columbus. However, there have been a number of challenges to the legality of the traffic cameras' use both through the courts and through the state legislature with bills introduced to overturn local legislation on the cameras. On his last day in office, former Ohio Governor Bob Taft vetoed a bill to overturn the use of the traffic cameras. The governor vetoed this bill because it contradicted the state's *Home Rule* law, which grants the power of self-government and to exercise certain police powers. In addition, the State Supreme Court upheld a ruling regarding the legality of cities' rights to enact legislation utilizing automated traffic-enforcement systems.

Politicizing an Otherwise Objective Process

Despite the traffic cameras' capacity to promote social equity and "level the playing field," rather than adhering to purely objective measures to determine the placement of the traffic cameras, the city's administration allowed the process to become politicized. This began with the mayor's initial announcement of the adoption of the use of traffic cameras in the city. With the city facing a $60 million budget deficit, which resulted in the layoff of up to 700 city employees in 2003, including 252 police officers and 70 firefighters, the mayor in office at the time, Jane Campbell, the city's first and only female mayor, misguidedly introduced the use of the traffic cameras as a means for the city to generate revenue rather than introducing it as proposed in the study, as a way of addressing the problem of racially biased ticketing and touting the safety enhancing capacity of the cameras' use. Research has shown that the use of traffic cameras in various jurisdictions across the country has resulted in a decrease in traffic accidents involving both vehicles and pedestrians at intersections with traffic cameras.[16]

There was aloud public outcry as citizens opposed the cameras, viewing their use as purely a money-making scheme to help solve the city's budget woes.

The mayor immediately attempted to modify her statement and promote the safety-enhancing aspects of the cameras as the primary objective behind their use. Unfortunately, it was too late. The damage had been done and the public perception of the cameras as principally a money-generating mechanism, that is, a "cash-cow," for the city had been established and persists to this day.[17]

In her efforts to rebrand the cameras' use however, the mayor did not mention the original intent behind the recommendation of the cameras—to address the racial bias in ticketing found in this study. The mayor did not acknowledge this aspect of the cameras' use until after five police-involved shootings of unarmed black men took place in the city, four resulting in fatalities, and three of which occurred within a one-month period at the end of the summer of 2005. In a community meeting at a black church in the neighborhood in which one of the police shootings occurred, in an effort to ease the heightened racial tension in the city's African American community as a result of the police shootings, the mayor publicly acknowledged for the first time that this study was the impetus for the traffic cameras' use and the original intent of their recommended use was to address the racial disparities in the traffic-ticketing patterns found throughout the city.[18]

The reluctance of the mayor, who defeated a black challenger to win the mayor's seat with roughly one-third of the black vote and maintained strong support in the African American community throughout her administration, to publicly promote the use of the traffic cameras as a means to address racially biased traffic-ticketing patterns found in the study was a political miscalculation and missed opportunity that could have potentially helped her win reelection in the 2006 mayoral race, which she lost to the African American president of City Council. As survey research on racial attitudes has consistently shown since the late 1950s, fewer white Americans hold and support racist views such as those associated with the racial segregation and discrimination of the Jim Crow era.[19] While research suggests that a social dissonance exists between the racial views that some whites espouse and their support for policies and programs designed to eradicate racial discrimination and disparities such as affirmative action, as noted few whites with the exception of those belonging to racial hate groups, are willing to publicly state views that promote racial inequality or that could be perceived as racist. Moreover, an astute politician of any race, particularly in a majority/minority city such as Cleveland, would be disinclined to publicly state their opposition to public policy initiatives designed to eradicate racial inequities that disproportionately affect that city's minority population. Therefore, had Mayor Campbell promoted the traffic cameras' capacity to address the issue of racial profiling while enhancing traffic safety she would have likely silenced any negative criticism she would have potentially received from her political opponents, for as Harris states, "right now in our society, there are few stronger epithets than racist"[20] and most, with the exception of the most ardent members of racial hate groups, are loath to be identified as such. Furthermore, a short time after the cameras had been in use she could have noted the revenue generated from the cameras as an unintended revenue stream that could be used to supplement the city's budget.

The camera placement process was further politicized when City Council members were allowed to oppose the placement of cameras at intersections in their wards. The city reportedly based the locations the cameras were placed on data indicating the number of accidents and tickets issued at the various locations as well as on-site traffic surveys, which were reportedly conducted at the selected sites. Despite the fact that some locations were among the top 30 sites identified by the city using this process some council members were able to keep cameras from being installed in their wards.[21] This interjected subjectivity into the process of determining the location of the cameras' placement. In addition, using the number of tickets issued at a given location as part of the criteria to determine the cameras placement was also problematic. As the analysis of the traffic-ticketing data in this study revealed, the traffic tickets in the city had been administered in a racially disparate manner. The first author of this research cautioned several African American members of the City Council, including the current mayor who was then the Council president, as well as the newly appointed chair of the public safety committee against allowing the placement of the cameras to be determined by the areas where a high volume of tickets had traditionally been issued, in that this would reinforce the racial disparities in ticketing that already existed. Nonetheless, this is what was allowed to happen as the majority of the cameras are located on the predominately black East Side of the city.

In spite of the progressive initiatives that the city took in implementing some of the recommendations from the study it failed to adopt one of the most important recommendations, that of passing legislation that prohibits the use of racial profiling by the police. Such legislation should also require the collection of racial traffic-ticketing data and the regular analysis and reporting of this data to be made available to the general public. These measures would provide for the systematic and uniform collection of racial demographic data on all traffic stops as well as enhance accountability and transparency to ensure that neither individual officers nor the department engages in practices of racially profiling or discrimination against any citizens either intentional or unintentionally. Legislation to address racial profiling was drafted by the first author working in conjunction with the Legal Redress Committee of the local chapter of the NAACP and an African American councilwoman who introduced the legislation to Council. However, the Council failed to enact the legislation but instead sent a resolution to the Ohio state legislature urging that body to adopt such legislation without acting upon it.

While such legislation could have been adopted at the local level and worked its way up to the state level, to date there is no legislation prohibiting racial profiling at the local or state level in Ohio. In addition, Ohio is one of only 16 states that do not have some form of racial profiling legislation enacted or pending either at the state or local level.[22]

In addition, while the city did move forward in implementing some of the recommendations from this study, the city did in fact commission another study of traffic-ticketing patterns which was referred to as a "Traffic Stop Data Collection Project." Consistent with the information provided by the high-ranking black police official prior to my meeting with the safety direction, this study was commissioned in July 2004, the same time period that media reports of this research first appeared. In fact, during my meeting with the safety director, he did inform me that a contract had been let for a study to look at traffic-ticketing patterns in the city. He stated that he would like to have me somehow be involved with the project, whether through a subcontracting role or in an advisory capacity. I was eventually informed that it was too late for me to be included in the contract work, but I was asked to serve on a Citizen's Contact Committee, which was to provide oversight of the Traffic Stop Data Collection Project, which I accepted.

By the time I joined the Citizen's Contact Committee the research methods and design of the study had already been determined. The committee was made up of a diverse cross-section of citizens from different racial, ethnic, and occupational backgrounds. There were elderly community members, religious leaders, merchants, and police officers from varying racial and ethnic backgrounds on the committee. I was the only academic researcher and the youngest person on the committee.

Upon learning of the data-collection methods which called for the use of a traffic stop form that was to be completed by police officers during each traffic stop whether a citation was administered or just a warning given, I asked him why weren't they using historic records, that is, traffic tickets, which could not be manipulated? To which he replied, "Because the racial demographic data on tickets was no longer being collected by the police department." According to the safety director, the chief (a white male) had stopped the required collection of racial demographic data on traffic tickets by officers, which the department had voluntarily began collecting in response to former Mayor Michael White's investigation of alleged organized racist activity within the police department, because as the chief stated, "we (the police department) do not racially profile and it (the collected racial demographic ticketing data) would only be used against white officers" (personal communication with the safety director).

This fact only reinforced the argument I had raised in a conversation with the then-president of City Council (and current mayor) regarding the need for legislation on racial profiling that prohibited the practice and mandated the collection of the racial demographic data. Such legislation would preclude the ability of any individual administrator to use his or her own discretion to determine whether or not the data were collected and it would provide standards for the collection and analysis of the data and penalties for those persons or agencies that failed to adhere to the legislation. He replied that he did not think that legislation was the only way to achieve the desired goal, indicating that a police directive or some other initiative within the political process could be used to accomplish the desired outcome. To the current mayor's credit, one of the very first actions he took upon being sworn into office was to issue a police policy directive. This directive addressed the deadly use of force by police and stated that the excessive and unnecessary use of deadly force would not be tolerated. And while this policy directive has significantly reduced the number of police-involved shootings, to date no policy directives or legislation regarding racial profiling or the mandatory collection of racial demographic ticketing data has been enacted.

I later posed the same question regarding the use of existing traffic-ticket data to one of the principal investigators of this second study at the first possible opportunity, when he came to town to brief the Citizen Contact Committee on the study's progress. When asked why they weren't using existing traffic-ticketing data to study the racial traffic-ticketing patterns rather than having the police collect data using the traffic stop forms, the investigator stated that they were interested in examining "what is happening currently rather than looking at what had happened in the past." The researcher appeared to take offense when I questioned the reliability of the data given the potential for *Hawthorne Effects, and* given the police officers' knowledge that they were involved in a study which sought to examine the issue of racial bias in traffic enforcement. After noting that my line of questioning was not welcomed by the researcher, and although there were other methodological concerns that I had during the implementation of the pilot and the actual study, I refrained from pressing the issue on the few occasions that the principal investigators were available to answer questions from the committee instead of their graduate research assistants. I decided to await the outcome of the study.

The final report of the Traffic Stop Data Collection Project was released in July of 2006. The findings of the study were determined to be "inconclusive" in that the data was "compromised."[23] Rather than completing the traffic stop data collection form for every traffic stop, police officers "either ticketed everyone they stopped or failed to document the motorists who didn't get tickets."[24]

In the study tickets were given in 97 percent of the 43,707 traffic stops. Nationally tickets are administered in only between 50 to 60 percent of all traffic stops. Blacks received 61.5 percent of the traffic tickets administered during the observation period, while whites received 30.5 percent of the citations, and Hispanics were 4.6 percent of those ticketed. See Table 8.1 below.

Despite the flaws in the study and the researchers' determination that the findings were "inconclusive" the data clearly show that blacks were the overwhelming majority of motorists ticketed. This study used both residential Census data and traffic observation data gathered in specific police zones as benchmarks to compare against the percentage of traffic tickets received by each racial group. While the questionable validity and reliability of the comparisons using both of these methods were cited, the researchers reported they had greater confidence in the data generated using traffic observations as the benchmark. Using these methods it was found that blacks were more than 1.5 times more likely to be stopped than whites in six out of nine police zones and blacks were more than 4 times more likely to be stopped than whites in two of these zones.[25] These findings are comparable to those from the earlier study of racial profiling in the city of Cleveland. The 61.5 percent of tickets received by blacks is greater than the 58 percent received by blacks in the earlier study. And using the percentage of tickets received by each racial group in the second study with the driving population estimates from the gravity model data used in the earlier study, blacks are 2.68 (61.5%/40%) times as likely to be ticketed by police in Cleveland than whites (30.5%/53% = 0.57). This is compared to the 2.13 likelihood of blacks being ticketed in comparison to whites found in our

TABLE 8.1   Traffic Stops and Tickets by Race from the Traffic Stop Data Collection Project

	Total	Blacks	Whites	Hispanics
Number of stops	43,707	26,879.81	13,330.64	2,010.52
Percentage of tickets per race	96.6%	61.5%	30.5%	4.6%
Total citations	42,220.96	25,965.89	12,877.39	1,942.16
Number of arrests		1,532.15	439.91	94.49
Percentage of arrests		5.7%	3.3%	4.7%

Chapter 8 | Epilogue: Research Study to Public Policy

earlier study. In spite of the problems noted with the consultants' study the disparities in ticketing observed in it were more egregious than those found in our earlier study.

The consultants' study also examined post–traffic stop outcomes and found that blacks and Hispanics were also more likely to have their cars searched than whites. Of the black motorists stopped by police 10.5 percent were either searched or had their vehicles searched, and 9 percent of Hispanics had either their person or vehicles searched, compared to 5.9 percent of white motorists. In addition, blacks and Hispanics were more likely to be arrested than whites, where 5.7 percent of blacks and 4.7 percent of Hispanics stopped by police were arrested compared to 3.3 percent of whites.

While the disparities in the rate at which blacks and Hispanics were searched and arrested were statistically significant, the consultants reported that after controlling for other legal or extralegal factors that might influence officers' decisions to search and arrest motorists, blacks and Hispanics were not significantly more likely to be arrested than whites while the likelihood of being searched remained significant for both groups. The authors explained that a number of situational or officer-level factors such as "being male, disrespectful, driving a vehicle in poor working condition, being stopped at night, etc."[26] accounted for the difference in the arrest rate among the racial/ethnic groups. Paradoxically, it is traffic stops based on such factors that are by definition the "pretextual stops" that are at the heart of the racial profiling debate.[27] While minorities of both genders report being the target of racial profiling, there is very little question that young black and Hispanic males are more likely to be the subject of increased police surveillance and investigative actions particularly in the context of the nation's more than 20-year "War on Drugs."

In addition, blacks and other minorities argue that equipment violations are among the alleged minor traffic infractions used by police as a guise to affect a traffic stop in order to execute further investigative procedures.[28] Furthermore, factors such as the motorist's demeanor or "being disrespectful" are things that the police officer cannot determine until after they've executed the stop. While being disrespectful to police officers during a police–citizen encounter is not advised and research does show that it increases the likelihood of being arrested, it is not an illegal offense, and what is perceived as disrespect by the officer is very likely a reaction to what is seen by the motorist as an unjustified or unwarranted traffic stop. These situational and officer level factors, which are highly subjective, do not adequately address the fundamental question in the racial profiling debate, "What was the reason for the traffic stop in the first place?"

EFFORTS TO CHANGE POLICING

While this study has had considerable influence on public policy which undoubtedly is due in no small part to serendipitous events and circumstances, it was also likely successful in being translated into policy because, while it identified racial disparities, it avoided making any particular individual or group responsible for these disparities. Moreover, it avoided labeling any persons or entities as "racist." This was achieved by focusing on the institutional manifestation of racism versus the individual perspective of racism, which most discussion of racial disparities generally digress to.

By focusing on institutional practices the study and policy recommendations put forth provided city leaders and law enforcement officials with measures to help ensure that fairness, equity, and integrity are an integral part of the manner in which the law is enforced, and that police interact with all members of the public. First, however, in order to achieve such outcomes, public officials, both those elected and those within law enforcement, must have the political will and fortitude to address sensitive and seemingly impenetrable issues such as racial profiling. Although scholars have conducted research that intersects race and policing for some time, criminal justice professionals, particularly the police, generally have not been receptive to such work.[29] Harris cites arguments raised by proponents of racial profiling that state" any extra enforcement effort that officers use against minorities results from common-sense application of probabilities, given who gets arrested everyday," to support his contention that police view research that investigates issues such as racial profiling as labeling "the law enforcement profession as a whole, or an individual police department, or perhaps some particular group of officers, as racist."[30]

What is at issue in this and similar studies are institutionalized practices that are often embodied in the informal policies that have been unwittingly passed on through generations of law enforcement officers and are manifest in racially discriminatory outcomes. Law enforcement officials should not simply dismiss such work as an attack on police as being "racist." Nor should they approach efforts to address racial and social inequities defensively but rather see it as an opportunity to address an issue that negatively impacts a significant and increasing portion of the American public which undermines the perception of legitimacy and trust in the police and the criminal justice system particularly within communities of color. Such reform efforts can serve to improve the relationship between the police and minority communities, particularly that with the African American community which has historically been strained.

Harris[31] cites research from the field of cognitive psychology[32] to explain that "most people harbor racial and ethnic biases on the unconscious level" and that "these unconsciously held biases operate independent of any consciously held beliefs and outside the awareness of those who hold them." Correll, Park, Judd, and Wittenbrink[33] conducted research examining the influence of implicit biases on a police officer's decision to shoot a person ostensibly threatening the officer with a deadly weapon. They found that the decision to shoot was made more quickly if the suspect was black and the decision to not shoot was made more quickly if the suspect was white. There was also found to be a strong shooter bias among those subjects who believed a pervasive racial stereotype in America of African Americans as aggressive and violent, which held regardless of the race of the subject. These studies indicate that most people in the United States, including police officers regardless of their race, are influenced by unconscious racial and ethnic biases.

In spite of the outwardly depressing implications of these studies' findings relative to reducing racial bias in policing, Summers and Ellsworth[34] found that "by making racial issues salient" subjects were less likely to act in a biased manner while Devine[35] found that "by consciously directing one's thought processes, one can overcome the influence of the automatically engaged biases and stereotypes that inhabit the unconscious."[36]

Therefore, it is essential that research such as this be used to illuminate the social and racial inequalities that exist within policing and the criminal justice system and make the decision makers within these institutions cognizant of the unconscious biases that set quiescent in the mind. Even though no individual is responsible for creating the circumstances from which racially biased outcomes such as those found in this study emanate, elected officials and law enforcement administrators, both black and white, at the top of these institutions and agencies must take responsibility and the lead in rectifying the inequities that exist.[37]

NOTES

1. The Cleveland traffic ticket studies in this book are based on a dissertation by Ronnie Dunn, "Spatial Profiling: To What Extent do the Cleveland Police Department's Traffic Ticketing Patterns Target Blacks?" Unpublished doctoral dissertation. Cleveland State University, Cleveland, OH.

2. G. C. Galster, & E. W. Hill (Eds.). *The Metropolis in Black & White: Place, Power, and Polarization* (Rutgers, NJ: The State University of New Jersey, 1992), pp. 173–174.

3. W. D. Keating, N. Krumholz, & D. C. Perry (Eds.) *Cleveland: A Metropolitan Reader* (Kent, OH: The Kent State University Press, 1995), p. 271.

4. Ibid., 278.

5. Ibid., 286–87.

6. Two Council seats were eliminated through referendum in 2009. The only seat on Council held by a Hispanic was consolidated with a neighboring white ward, which was won by the white incumbent. And two black wards were consolidated and the vacant seat held by an interim Council person was won by the black incumbent from the neighboring ward.

7. M. F. Rice (Ed.). *Diversity and Public Administration: Theory, Issues, and Perspectives* (Armonk, NY: M. E. Sharpe, 2005).

8. Ibid.

9. R. Brett (June 30, 2004). Tale of Two Roads Reveals Racial Divide. *The Plain Dealer*, p. B1.

10. R. Brett (July 9, 2004). Tickets for One and All. *The Plain Dealer*, p. B1.

11. The safety director became a regular guest lecturer in the undergraduate urban studies class of the principal investigator, speaking each semester during the remainder of his tenure as the city's safety director. In addition, the principal investigator personally observed increased traffic patrols along this thoroughfare immediately after the study was released.

12. A request for public records of the traffic camera tickets was submitted to the city in 2007 in order to conduct an analysis of the racial distribution of the traffic tickets. To date, this request has not been met. Although race is not noted on the camera tickets, the city of Cleveland and the surrounding communities within Cuyahoga County are so hyper-segregated that the address of the motorist the vehicle is registered to can be used as a proxy for race (see Meehan & Ponder, 2004).

13. These figures were computed using residential demographic data from the 2000 Census Bureau Geographic Comparison Tables for Cuyahoga County Ohio. The driving age thresholds used in this computation were 15 through 84 years of age. There were no driving-age residents of other races identified in the datasets.

14. J. Horton (February 3, 2009). "Don't Forget to Smile as Camera Busts You: Cleveland's Got a Moneymaker on the East Side," *The Plain Dealer*.

15. D. Summers (January 13, 2009). WKYC TV 3 News Report.

16. F. M. Council, B. Persaud, K. Eccles, C. Lyon, & M. S. Griffith (2005). *Safety Evaluation of Red-Light Cameras*. McLean, VA.: U.S. Department of Transportation Federal Highway Administration; C. M. Cunningham, & J. S. Hummer *Evaluating the Use of Red Light Running Photographic Enforcement Using Collisions and Red Light Running Violations* (Raleigh, N.C.: Institute of Transportation Research and Education, 2004).

17. P. Morris (January 5, 2010). "It's About Time for Cleveland Mayor Frank Jackson to Show Signs of Fear or Panic," *The Plain Dealer*.

18. _____ (October 11, 2005). "Reviving Trust Will Take More Than a Taser," *The Plain Dealer*.

19. E. Bonilla-Silva *Racism without Racists* (New York: Rowman & Littlefield Publishers, 2006); D. A. Harris (August 2007). "The Importance of Research on Race and Policing: Making Race Salient to Individuals and Institutions with

Criminal Justice." University of Pittsburgh Law School. *Legal Studies Research Paper Series*, Working Paper No. 2007-5.

20. Harris, "The Importance of Research on Race and Policing," p. 5.

21. O. Perkins (June 7, 2005). "City Picks Intersections for Cameras, *The Plain Dealer*, pp. A1 & A7.

22. "The Racial Profiling Data Collection Resource Center," available at http://www .racialprofilinganalysis.neu.edu/.

23. R. Brett (August 6, 2006). "More Questions after Police Study," *The Plain Dealer*, p. B1; S. Vinella, & G. Baird (August 5, 2006). "Police Balked at Study, Researchers Say," *The Plain Dealer*, pp. B1 & B5.

24. Brett, "More Questions after Police Study.

25. R. S. Engel, J. Frank, R. Tillyer, & C. Klahm *Cleveland Division of Police Traffic Stop Data Study: Final Report* (Cincinnati: University of Cincinnati, Division of Criminal Justice, 2006).

26. Ibid., p. xiii.

27. R. A. Dunn (2009). "Measuring Racial Disparities in Traffic Ticketing Within Large Urban Jurisdictions," *Public Performance & Management Review 32*(4): pp. 537–559.

28. Harris, "The Importance of Research on Race and Policing."

29. Ibid.

30. Ibid., p. 5.

31. Ibid.

32. P. G. Devine (1989). "Stereotypes and Prejudice: Their Automatic and Controlled Components," *Journal of Personality and Social Psychology 56*, pp. 5–18; S. R. Sommers, & P. C. Ellsworth (2000). "Race in the Courtroom: Perceptions of Guilt and Dispositional Attributions," *Personality and Social Psychology Bulletin 26*, 1367–1379; S. R. Sommers, & P. C. Ellsworth (2001). "White Juror Bias: An Investigation of Prejudice against Black Defendants in the American Courtroom," *Psychology, Public Policy, and Law 7*, pp. 201–229; A. G. Greenwald, & M. R. Banaji (2007). "Implicit Social Cognition: Attitudes, Self-Esteem, and Stereotypes," *Psychological Review 102*, pp. 4–27.

33. Harris, "The Importance of Research on Race and Policing."

34. Sommers & Ellsworth, "White Juror Bias."

35. Devine, "Stereotypes and Prejudice."

36. Harris, "The Importance of Research on Race and Policing."

37. Dunn, "Measuring Racial Disparities in Traffic Ticketing Within Large Urban Jurisdictions."

CONCLUSION

Our examination of racial profiling has focused on the driving while black (DWB) phenomenon, a significant and problematic issue in the lives of many African Americans. Our primary objectives have been to demonstrate the existence of racial profiling in this law enforcement practice and the systematic nature of this form of racism. In addition we wanted to illuminate some of the harmful consequences of racial profiling.

Many studies and reports show that African American and Hispanic motorists are stopped by police officers at higher rates than white drivers. Both of the African American authors of this book have been stopped and/or been an object of police surveillance multiple times. This treatment cuts across all classes of African Americans, especially males. Olgletree[1] reported the words of 100 prominent and professional black males describing one of their DWB moments. Some of these men are well known, all were established professionals, and each had been subjected to harsh racial profiling. And if men of such supposed class stature are treated in this manner, we can only imagine how black men and boys from working-, lower-, and underclass backgrounds across the country are treated.

One of the issues in studying the traffic ticketing aspect of the DWB issue is how best to measure the numerator and the denominator for the analysis. Often the numerator is the number of tickets issued by race during a set period of time in a specific geographic area. Data used for the denominator varies. Some studies use census data to indicate the demographics of the population in the area studied. Others use state Department of Motor Vehicle (DMV) data to estimate the proportions of licensed drivers by race. We improved on these methods by using the gravity model, a method used in transportation planning and travel demand forecasting. It estimates the number of motorists by race, including all drivers, whether residents of the area or not. With this approach we found that blacks received a disproportionate share of tickets in Cleveland, Ohio, in general, and in specific areas of the city, in particular. Of course, these kind of analyses can demonstrate disparities in ticketing but not racial discrimination, as it may be unknown whether such disparate ticketing is warranted. In other words, blacks may commit proportionately more traffic violations than whites in the area being investigated. This must be ascertained before racial discrimination can be asserted.

We used official ticketing data as the numerator and conducted traffic censuses to determine the racial makeup of the motorists on the thoroughfares. Further, a radar gun was used to measure the speed of motorists by race to determine the appropriate rate of ticketing. With these methods we demonstrated that the law enforcement practices examined constituted racial discrimination, as there was no criminal justice reason for blacks being stopped and ticketed at higher rates than whites. Harris[2] has shown this lack of support for the excess rate of stops of black motorists. He reported on the hit rates from studies of traffic stops and searches in Maryland, New Jersey, and North Carolina, which revealed that in each of these states contraband (guns or drugs) were found at higher rates in the cars of white motorists than black motorists. In our analysis of stop, yield, and search data from 13 states it was found that blacks and Hispanics are stopped at higher rates than whites and they are also searched at higher rates. Yet the yield rates in the majority of these states were higher for white motorists than black or Hispanic motorists. More blacks and Hispanics than whites are arrested because substantially more of them are stopped and searched. However, more would not be arrested if all motorists were stopped and searched at equal rates, or at the rates suggested by the yields.

INSTITUTIONAL RACISM

In our study in Cleveland, motorists on the street with predominantly black motorists, Kinsman, were more frequently sanctioned for traffic violations than motorists traveling on the majority white driver thoroughfare, Chester. Although Kinsman had substantially fewer vehicles per day than Chester, drivers on Kinsman received nearly 4 times the number of tickets as drivers on Chester.

Given the predominantly black driving population on Kinsman the over-whelming majority of those ticketed on this street were black. While blacks on Kinsman were ticketed at approximately the same rate as their proportion of drivers on this street, they were disproportionately ticketed on Chester, the street with the majority of white drivers. This occurred despite blacks having fewer drivers and lower speeds on the street.

By studying the police department's formal and informal practices we were able to demonstrate that the traffic enforcement practices were in effect spatial profiling. The institutionalized standards of practice resulted in different procedures for blacks and whites. More police cars were assigned to the thoroughfare where blacks were the predominant users than the street where the majority of users were white. This practice persisted even though the majority white thoroughfare had substantially more traffic and higher speeds. These deployment practices had been in place for many years; and they worked consistently to the disadvantage of black motorists. Consequently, the practice is institutional racism, as blacks received more tickets than their fair share. This is racism. If racist consequences result from an institution's laws, customs, or practices, that institution is racist whether or not the individuals maintaining those practices have racist intentions.

While not totally discounting individual police officers' use of discretion in stops and ticketing, the traffic enforcement deployment patterns reduce the significance of the race of the officers and the relevance of police discretion in this racial profiling. We demonstrate the institutional nature of the DWB issue as a more appropriate approach than the traditional individual racist police officer paradigm in which the issue is generally discussed. Aside from being a more accurate assessment of the situation, the institutional approach has more utility. By shifting the impetus of the discussion of racism from the individual to the institution the personal burden of being labeled a "racist" and the usual resulting resistance to addressing the issue should be diminished.

Whether the issue is DWB or the killing of unarmed black men, the discussion often tends to center around the notion of "rogue" cops, rather than systemic racism. This approach tends to characterize these acts as aberrant, the result of "bad apples." This kind of approach treats racism as a random event that occurs by the whim of a racist cop, if it does occur at all. This is a misreading of social phenomena. Many observers, when reminded of the "olden days," of more overt racial oppression of African Americans, will readily understand the systematic nature of how the criminal justice system was used in that endeavor. Our effort here is to note that unless all of the racist activities of criminal justice systems have been eradicated since the "olden days," they will still be operable, regardless of the intentions, orientations, and the race or ethnicity of the leaders of that system.

CONSEQUENCES

Racial profiling has many consequences for African Americans. One consequence is a psychological effect. The increase in racial profiling increases the surveillance of African Americans. Glover[3] writes about the psychological effects of this surveillance. One of her young black male interviewees described racial profiling as psychological warfare and compared the constant surveillance to the "governance of the body" during slavery.

Our focus has been on DWB. While the act of racial profiling is much broader than stopping and searching the vehicles of black motorists, it is exemplary of the broader phenomenon, and it can lead to more serious situations. Disproportionate ticketing predisposes black males to increased contact with the criminal justice system, which can result in their deeper involvement with the system. And of course the stops and searches can result in arrests and imprisonment at higher rates for blacks than their proportion of violators would call for.

This disproportionate searching of vehicles driven by blacks is a part of what some observers dub "the war on blacks," rather than the "war on drugs." Over one-third of all U.S. prisoners are incarcerated for drug charges. For example, blacks are 14 percent of the users of illegal drugs and they are a similar percentage of the drug dealers. However, they are 34 percent of those arrested for drugs, 53 percent of those convicted, and 63 of those incarcerated for drugs.[4]

One of the most significant effects of a prison record is diminished employment prospects. The stigma of the felony conviction reduces employability for many employers. In addition, there are state restrictions on employment in some areas and in licensing, even in some jobs that have no discernible crime control issues. The consequences of felony records may have become greater in recent decades. As a part of the so-called "war on drugs," federal law penalizes persons with felony drug convictions. For example there are currently significant restrictions on access to welfare benefits, public housing, and financial aid for higher education.[5]

Large-scale incarceration is also resulting in increased negative health consequences. There has been a rapid spread of tuberculosis, and there has been an increase of HIV infection among many inmates. This is because many drug offenders are incarcerated, and some tend to engage in intravenous drug use, share needles, and/or trade sex for drugs.[6]

One of the most devastating statistics is that one-third of all young black males, men in the age group 20 to 29, are in the criminal justice system. This is the decade of life when youth transition into adulthood. During this time they tend to finish their education and get situated in a regular occupation, which often leads to marriage and a family. This transition is seriously compromised by felony convictions, which make employment problematic. The increasing occurrence of felony records and problematic employment is causing the proportion of black marriageable mates to decrease, thus affecting black families, and among other things, influencing increases in lone mother households.

Another negative consequence of the high involvement of black males with the criminal justice system is the loss of voting rights. In many states individuals with felony records lose the right to vote. There are over 2 million African Americans in that situation. They are 38 percent of the total number of 5.3 million such disfranchised individuals in the country. Some 13 percent of all African American men are denied the vote on this basis. In some states up to one-third of the entire African American male population are denied the vote. At the current rate of incarceration, one-third of the next generation of black men will be denied the right to vote. In other words they will lose their principal citizen right.[7]

Alexander[8] calls the current functioning of the criminal justice system "the new Jim Crow," arguing that it performs similar functions to the old Jim Crow, the era from the late 19th century to the 1960's, when ostensibly the era of legalized racial oppression was ended. However, as she notes,

Like Jim Crow, mass incarceration marginalizes large segments of the African American community, segregates them physically (in prisons, jails, and ghettos), and then authorizes discrimination against them in voting, employment, housing, education, public benefits, and jury service. The federal court system has effectively immunized the current system from challenges on the grounds of racial bias, much as earlier systems of control were protected and endorsed by the U.S. Supreme Court.

SOLUTIONS

The move toward solutions will not be speedy or effective until and unless there is an increased realization that racism is systemic as well as individual. It is not just a matter of individual bias. When we shift the emphasis from "bad cops" to policies and practices we will begin to move toward solutions. When the emphasis is on policies and practices there is potentially less finger-pointing and individual officials bracing against being called "racist."

Of course, there must be a recognition that racial disparities exist in the criminal justice system. The collection and analysis of data would facilitate the determination of whether these disparities are the result of racially discriminatory activities. However, less than one-third of the states collect data on traffic stops that are sufficient for this task. At a minimum we must begin to collect the necessary type of data. Then we can move on to examining and rectifying inequities in other aspects of the criminal justice system.

NOTES

1. C. Olgletree. *The Presumption of Guilt: The Arrest of Henry Louis Gates and Race, Class, and Crime in America* (New York: Palgrave Macmillan, 2010).

2. D. Harris, D. *Profiles in Injustice: Why Racial Profiling Cannot Work* (New York: The New Press, 2002).

3. K. S. Glover. *Racial Profiling: Research, Racism, and Resistance* (Lanham: Rowman & Littfield, 2009).

4. Human Rights Watch (2003). *Incarcerated America*. Available at http://hrw.org/backgrounder/usa/incarceration/.

5. M. Mauer. *Race to Incarcerate* (New York: The New Press, 2006).

6. Ibid.

7. Legal Defense Fund (2010). *Free the Vote: Unlocking Democracy in the Cells and on the Streets*. Available at http://naacpldf.org/files/publications/Free%20the%20Vote.pdf.

8. M. Alexander. *The New Jim Crow: Mass Incarceration in the Age of Colorblindness* (New York: The New Press, 2010).

BIBLIOGRAPHY

ACLU and Rights Working Group. 2009. *The Persistence of Racial and Ethnic Profiling in the United States 40.*

Alexander, M. 2010. *The New Jim Crow: Mass Incarceration in the Age of Colorblindness.* New York: The New Press.

American Psychiatric Association. 1994. *Diagnostic and Statistical Manual of Mental Disorders,* 4th ed. Washington, DC: APA.

Anderson, E. 2000. *Code of the Street: Decency, Violence, and the Moral Life of the Inner City.* New York: W.W. Norton.

Anderson, E. 1990. *Streetwise.* Chicago: University of Chicago Press.

Antonovics, K., and B. G. Knight. February 2009. A New Look at Racial Profiling: Evidence from the Boston Police Department. *The Review of Economics and Statistics* 91(1): 163–177.

Barandes, L., T. Loftus, P. Segner, and J. Sweeney. 2004. "A Pattern of Suspicion: Dateline Investigates Claims of Racial Profiling." US: MSNBC.com.

Beimborn, E., and R. Kennedy. 1996. *Inside the Blackbox: Making Transportation Models Work For Livable Communities.* Madison, WI: University of Wisconsin–Milwaukee.

Black, D. 1976. *The Behavior of Law.* New York: Academic Press.

Bonczar, T. P. 2003. Prevalence of Imprisonment in the U.S. Population. 1974–2001. Washington, DC: Bureau of Justice Statistics.

Bonilla-Silva, E. 2006. *Racism without Racists.* New York: Rowman & Littlefield Publishers.

Bouza, A. V. 2001. *Police Unbound: Corruption, Abuse, and Heroism by the Boys in Blue.* Amherst, NY: Prometheus Books.

Brett, R. 2004. Tale of Two Roads Reveals Racial Divide. *The Plain Dealer,* June 30, 2004, p. B1.

Brett, R. 2004. Tickets for One and All. *The Plain Dealer,* July 9, 2004, p. B1.

Brett, R. 2006. More Questions after Police Study. *The Plain Dealer,* August 6, 2006, p. B1.

Carmichael, S., and C. Hamilton. 1967. *Black Power: The Politics of Liberation in America.* New York: Random House.

Carroll, J. D. 1955. Spatial Interactions and the Urban-Metropolitan Description. *Traffic Quarterly,* 149–161.

"Citizen Stops." 2002. Cleveland: General Police Order Cleveland Division of Police.

Clark, M. D. 2009. Testimony: Hearing before the General Court of the Commonwealth of Massachusetts Joint Committee on the Judiciary, October 27, 2009.

Cook, W. 1967. Policemen in Society: Which Side Are They On? *Berkeley Journal of Sociology 12*: p. 13.

Cordner, G., B. Williams, and A. Velasco. 2002. *Vehicle Stops in San Diego: 2001 (Report).* San Diego, CA.: Eastern Kentucky University; Vanderbilt University; San Diego State University.

Cordner, G., B. Williams, and M. Zuniga. 2000. *Vehicle Stop Study: Mid-year Report.* San Diego, CA.: San Diego Police Department.

Council, F. M., Persaud, B., Eccles, K., Lyon, C., and Griffith, M. S. 2005. Safety Evaluation of Red-Light Cameras. McLean, VA.: U.S. Dept. of Transportation Federal Highway Administration.

Cunningham, C. M., and Hummer, J. S. 2004. Evaluating the Use of Red Light Running Photographic Enforcement Using Collisions and Red Light Running Violations. Raleigh, NC.: Institute of Transportation Research and Education.

Davis, K. C. 1975. *Police Discretion.* St. Paul, MN: West Publishing Co.

Devine, P. G. 1989. Stereotypes and Prejudice: Their Automatic and Controlled Components. *Journal of Personality and Social Psychology 56,* 5–18.

Dunn, R. A. 2004. Spatial Profiling: To What Extent Do the Cleveland Police Department's Traffic Ticketing Patterns Disproportionately Target Blacks? (Doctoral Dissertation, Cleveland State University, 2004; UMI No. 072699).

Dunn, R. A. 2009. Measuring Racial Disparities in Traffic Ticketing Within Large Urban Jurisdictions. *Public Performance & Management Review* 32(4): pp. 537–559.

Dunn, R. A. 2010. Race and the Relevance of Citizen Complaintants Against the Police. *Administrative Theory & Praxis* (in press).

Engel, R. S., J. Frank, R. Tillyer, and C. Klahm. 2006. *Cleveland Division of Police Traffic Stop Data Study: Final Report*. Cincinnati: University of Cincinnati, Division of Criminal Justice.

Farrell, A., J. McDevitt, S. Cronin, and E. Pierce. 2003. Rhode Island Traffic Stop Statistics Act, Final Report. Boston: Northeastern University, Institute of Race and Justice.

Feagin, J. 2000. *Racist America: Roots, Current Realities, and Future Reparations*. New York: Routledge.

Fellner, J. 2009. "Race, Drugs, and Law Enforcement in the United States." *Stanford Law & Policy Review* 20(2): pp. 257–291.

Foucault, M. 1977. *Discipline & Punish: The Birth of the Prison*. New York: Vintage Books.

Fridell, L. A. 2004. By the Numbers: A Guide for Analyzing Race Data from Vehicle Stops. Washington, D.C.: Police Executive Research Forum.

Fridell, L. A., R. Lunney, D. Diamond, B. Kubu, M. Scott, and C. Laing. 2001. *Racially Biased Policing: A Principled Response*. Washington, D.C.: Police Executive Research Forum.

Galliher, J. 1971. Explanations of Police Behavior. *Sociological Quarterly* 12: p. 11.

Galster, G. C., and E. W. Hill, eds. 1992. *The Metropolis in Black & White: Place, Power, and Polarization*. Rutgers, NJ: State University of New Jersey.

Georges-Abeyie, D. E., ed. 1984. *The Criminal Justice System and Blacks*. New York: C. Boardman Co.

Ginsberg, T., and H. Goldman. 1999. "Firing of NJ Police Superintendent Adds Fuel to Racial Profiling Debate." *Knight Ridder/Tribune News Service*, March 2, 1999.

Glover, K. S. 2009. *Racial Profiling: Research, Racism, and Resistance*. Lanham: Rowman & Littlefield Publishers.

Gordon, C., ed. 1980. *Power/Knowledge: Selected Interviews and Other Writings 1972–1977 Michel Foucault*. New York: Pantheon Books, 1980.

Greenwald, A. G., and M. R. Banaji. 1995. "Implicit Social Cognition: Attitudes, Self-Esteem, and Stereotypes." *Psychological Review* 102: 4–27.

Hagan, J., and R. Dinovitzer. 1999. Collateral Consequences of Imprisonment for Children, Communities, and Prisoners. *Crime and Justice*, Vol. 26, Prisons, p. 122.

Harris, D. 1999. *Driving While Black: Racial Profiling on Our Nation's Highways*. New York: ACLU Department of Public Education.

Harris, D. A. 2005. *Good Cop: The Case for Preventive Policing*. New York: The New Press.

Harris, D. A. 2007. The Importance of Research on Race and Policing: Making Race Salient to Individuals and Institutions with Criminal Justice. University of Pittsburgh Law School. Legal Studies Research Paper Series, Working Paper No. 2007-5.

Harris, D. 1998. "Particularized Suspicion, Categorical Judgments: Supreme Court Rhetoric Versus Lower Court Reality under *Terry v. Ohio*." *St. John's Law Review* 72: 1.

Harris, D. 1999. Personal communication.

Harris, D. 2002. *Profiles in Injustice: Why Racial Profiling Cannot Work*. New York: The New Press.

Harris, D. 1999. "The Stories, the Statistics, and the Law: Measuring Driving While Black." *Minnesota Law Review* 84: 265–317.

Hayes, P. 1999. *Blacklisted: An investigation of racial profiling*. WKYC Television News: US.

Hernandez-Murillo, R., and J. Knowles. 2004. Racial Profiling or Racist Policing? Bounds Tests in Aggregate Data. *International Economic Review* 45(3): pp. 959–989.

Horton, J. 2009. "Don't Forget to Smile as Camera Busts You: Cleveland's Got a Moneymaker on the East Side." *The Plain Dealer*, February 3, 2009, p. A2.

Human Rights Watch. 2003. *Incarcerated America*. http://hrw.org/backgrounder/usa/incarceration/.

Human Rights Watch. 2000. *Punishment and Prejudice: Racial Disparities in the War on Drugs*. http://www.hrw.org/reports/2000/usa/.

Ireland, J., and D. H. Weinberg with E. Steinmetz. 2002. Racial and Ethnic Residential Segregation in the United States: 1980–2000. Washington, DC: U.S. Government Printing Office, p. 438.

Keating, W. D., N. Krumholz, and D. C. Perry, ed. 1995. *Cleveland: A Metropolitan Reader*. Kent, OH: Kent State University Press.

Knowles, L., and K. Prewitt, eds., 1969. *Institutional Racism in America*. Englewood Cliffs, NJ: Prentice Hall.

Kusmer, K. L. 1976. *A Ghetto Takes Shape*. Urbana and Chicago: University of Illinois Press.

Lamberth, J. 1996. *State of New Jersey v. Pedro Soto*, 324 N. J. Super. 66; 734 A.2d 350; 1996 N. J. Super. Lexis 554.

Langan, P. A., L. A. Greenfeld, S. K. Smith, M. R. Durose, and D. J. Levin, 2001. *Police–Public Contact Survey*. Washington, DC: U.S. Department of Justice.

Legal Defense Fund. 2010. *Free the Vote: Unlocking Democracy in the Cells and on the Streets*. http://naacpldf.org/files/publications/Free%20the%20Vote.pdf.

Liderbach, J., C. R. Trulson, E. J. Fritsch, T. J. Caeti, and R. W. Taylor. 2007. Racial Profiling and the Political Demand for Data: A Pilot Study Designed to Improve Methodologies in Texas. *Criminal Justice Review* 32(2): pp. 101–120.

Massey, D. S., and N. A. Denton. 1993. *American Apartheid*. Cambridge: Harvard University Press.

Mauer, M. 1997. *Intended and Unintended Consequences: State Racial Disparities in Imprisonment*. Washington, DC: The Sentencing Project.

Mauer, M. 2006. *Race to Incarcerate*. New York: The New Press.

Mauer, M. 2009. *Racial Disparities in the Criminal Justice System: Testimony Prepared for the House Judiciary Subcommittee on Crime, Terrorism, and Homeland Security*. October 29, 2009. Washington, DC: The Sentencing Project.

Mauer, M., and T. Huling. 1995. *Intended and Unintended Consequences: State Racial Disparities in Imprisonment*. Washington, DC: The Sentencing Project.

The Mayor's Investigative Report on Racism Within the Cleveland Police Department. 1999. Cleveland: Mayor's Office.

Meehan, A., and M. Ponder. 2002. Race and Place: The Ecology of Racial Profiling African American Motorists. *Justice Quarterly* 19(3): pp. 399–430.

Miller, J. G. 1996. *Search and Destroy: African-American Males in the Criminal Justice System*. New York: Cambridge University Press.

Milovanovic, D., and K. Russell, eds. 2001. *Petit Apartheid in the U.S. Criminal Justice System*. Durham, NC: Carolina Academic Press.

Minton, T. 2010. *Jail Inmates at Midyear 2009—Statistical Tables*. Bureau of Justice Statistics.

http://bjs.ojp.usdoj.gov/content/pub/pdf/jim09st.pdf

Moore, L. N. 2003. *Carl B. Stokes and the Rise of Black Political Power*. Urbana and Chicago: University of Illinois Press, p. 27.

Morgan, G. 1986. *Images of Organization*. Thousand Oaks, CA: Sage Publications.

Morris, P. 2010. "It's About Time for Cleveland Mayor Frank Jackson to Show Signs of Fear or Panic." *The Plain Dealer*, January 5, 2010, B1.

National Conference of State Legislatures. 2001. *State Laws Address "Racial Profiling."* Washington, DC: National Conference of State Legislatures.

"Ohio Revised Code Title XLV Motor Vehicles, Aeronautics, Watercraft, Driver's License Suspension, Cancellation, Revocation." In *Chapter 4510*, Sec. 0.3.07.

Olgletree, C. 2010. *The Presumption of Guilt: The Arrest of Henry Louis Gates Jr. and Race*. New York: Palgrave MacMillan.

Oliver, M. L., and Shapiro, T. 1997. *Black Wealth/White Wealth*. London: Routledge.

Osinsky, D. M. 1996. *"Worse than Slavery": Parchman Farm and the Ordeal of Jim Crow*. New York: Free Press Paperbacks.

Pager, D. 2003. The Mark of a Criminal Record. *American Journal of Sociology* 108(5): pp. 937–75.

Park, R. 1925. *The City: Suggestions for the Investigation of Human Behaviour*. Chicago: University of Chicago Press.

Patton, S. 2009. America on Lockdown: New Facts about America's Prisons & Prisoners. Legal Defense Fund. http://www.thedefendersonline.com/2009/02/03/america–on–lockdown–new–facts–about–america%E2%80%99s–prisons–prisoners/

Petrocelli, M., A. Piquero, and M. Smith. 2003. Conflict theory and racial profiling: An empirical analysis of police traffic stop data. *Journal of Criminal Justice* 31(1): pp. 1–11.

Perkins, O. 2005. City Picks Intersections for Cameras. *The Plain Dealer*, June 7, 2005, pp. A1 & A7.

Rajchman, J. 1991. *Foucault's Art of Seeing, in Philosophical Events: Essays of the 80s*. New York: Columbia University Press.

Ramirez, D., J. McDevitt, and A. Farrell. 2000. *A Resource Guide on Racial Profiling Data Collection Systems*. Boston: Northeastern University.

Report of the National Advisory Commission on Civil Disorders. 1968. New York: Bantam Books.

Rice, M. F. (Ed.) 2005. *Diversity and Public Administration: Theory, Issues, and Perspectives.* Armonk, NY: M.E. Sharpe.

Roberts, D. E. 2001. *Criminal Justice and Black Families: The Collateral Damage of Over-Enforcement.* U.C. Davis L. Rev. 1005.

Rosich, K. 2007. *Race, Ethnicity, and the Criminal Justice System.* Washington, DC: American Sociological Association. http://asanet.org.

Salling, M., 2001. *Cleveland Neighborhood Conditions and Trends.* Cleveland: Maxine Goodman-Levin College of Urban Affairs.

Sanchez-Hucles, J. 1999. "Racism: Emotional; Abusiveness and Psychological Trauma for Ethnic Minorities." *Journal of Emotional Abuse* (2): pp. 69–87.

Schockley, S. M. 1999. "Another Face of DWB: Are Southeast Clevelanders Targeted for Speed Traps?" *Cleveland Life,* June 16, 1999, p. 1.

Scholz, K. 1999. "Chief Warns Police: Issue Tickets or Else." *The Plain Dealer,* September 24, 1999, p. 21.

Scholz, K. 1999. "Police Pick up the Pace on Tickets: Six-Week Drop in Citations Issued Ends." *The Plain Dealer,* October 2, 1999, p. 12.

Schrantz, D. 2000. *Reducing Racial Disparity in the Criminal Justice System.* Washington, DC: The Sentencing Project.

The Sentencing Project. 1997. *Crack Cocaine Sentencing Policy: Unjustified and Unreasonable.* Washington, DC: The Sentencing Project.

The Sentencing Project. 2007. "Facts About Prisons and Prisoners." http://www.sentencingproject.org.

The Sentencing Project. 2010. Racial Disparity. http://www.sentencingproject.org/template/page .cfm?id=122

Siegal and Senna. 1997. *Juvenile Delinquency.* St. Paul, MN: West Publishing Company.

Smith, D. A. V., C. A. 1981. Street-level justice: Situational Determinants of Police Arrest Decisions. *Social Problems* 29(2): p. 11.

Smith, M. R., and G. P. Alpert. 2002. "Searching for Direction: Courts, Social Science, and the Adjudication of Racial Profiling Claims." *Justice Quarterly* 19(4).

Smith, M. R., and M. Petrocelli. 2001. "Racial Profiling? A Multivariate Analysis of Police Traffic Stop Data." *Police Quarterly* 4: 4–27.

Smith, R. L., and D. Davis. 2002. "Migration Patterns Hold Back Cleveland: Segregation Takes Economic Toll, Analysts Say." *The Plain Dealer,* p. 8.

Sommers, S. R., and P. C., Ellsworth. 2000. Race in the Courtroom: Perceptions of Guilt and Dispositional attributions. *Personality and Social Psychology Bulletin, 26,* 1367–1379.

Sommers, S. R., and P. C. Ellsworth. 2001. White Juror Bias: An Investigation of Prejudice against Black Defendants in the American Courtroom. *Psychology, Public Policy, and Law, 7,* 201–229.

Strom, K. J., and M. R. Durose. 2001. *Traffic Stop Data Collection Policies for State Police, 2001.* Washington, D.C.: Bureau of Justice Statistics, U.S. Department of Justice.

Sugrue, T. J. 2005. "Driving While Black: The Car and Race Relations in Modern America," *Automobile in American Life and Society.* Dearborn: Henry Ford Museum and University of Michigan. http://www.autolife.umd.umich.edu.

Summers, D. 2009. WKYC TV 3 News Report. January 13, 2009.

Terry v. Ohio. Symposium Issue. 1998. *St. John's Law Review* 72: p. 826.

Tucker, M. B., and C. Mitchell-Kernan. 1995. *The Decline in Marriage Among African Americans.* New York: Russell Sage Foundation.

Turner, K. 2000. "Cleveland Police Data Are Unclear on Profiling." *The Plain Dealer,* August 15, 2000, p. 4.

Turner, K. 2003. "A Lawman's Legacy." *The Plain Dealer Sunday Magazine,* October 26, 2003, 12–18.

Vinella, S., and G. Baird. 2006. Police Balked at Study, Researchers Say. *The Plain Dealer,* August 5, 2006, pp. B1 & B5.

Wacquant, L. 2001. *Deadly Symbiosis: When Ghetto and Prison Meet and Merge.* Thousand Oaks, CA: Sage.

Walker, S. 2003. *Internal Benchmarking for Traffic Stop Data: An Early Intervention System Approach.* Paper presented at the conference, Confronting Racial Profiling in the 21st Century, Boston, MA.

Walker, S. 2005. *The New World of Police Accountability.* London: Sage Publications.

Walker, S. 2001. *Police Accountability: The Role of Citizen Oversight.* Belmont, CA: Wadsworth Group.

Websdale, N. 2001. *Policing the Poor.* Boston: Northeastern University Press.

West, H. 2010. *Prison Inmates at Midyear 2009–Statistical Tables.* Bureau of Justice Statistics. http://bjs.ojp.usdoj.gov/index.cfm?ty=pb detail&iid=2200

Whren v. United States. 1995. 517 U.S. 806.

Wilbanks, W. 1987. *Myth of a Racist Criminal Justice System.* Monterey, CA: Brooks/Cole Publishing.

Wilkins, R. L. 2000. Testimony of Robert L. Wilkins, concerning "The Traffic Stops Statistics Study Act of 1999," before the Committee on the Judiciary Subcommittee on the Constitution, Federalism and Property Rights, United States Senate, March 30, 2000, p. 2.

Wilson, W. J. 1987. *The Truly Disadvantaged: The Inner City, the Underclass, and Public Policy.* Chicago: University of Chicago Press.

Wilson, W. J. 1996. *When Work Disappears: The World of the New Urban Poor.* New York: Knopf.

Wintersmith, R. F. 1974. *The Police and the Black Community.* Lexington, MA: Lexington Books.

Zingraff, M., H. Mason, W. R. Smith, D. Devey-Tomaskovic, P. Warren, H. L. McMurray, and C. R. Fenton. 2000. *Evaluating North Carolina State Highway Patrol Data: Citations, Warnings, and Searches in 1998.* Report submitted to North Carolina Department of Crime Control and Public Safety and North Carolina State Highway.

Ronnie Dunn, Ph. D., is associate professor of urban studies at the Maxine Goodman-Levin College of Urban Affairs at Cleveland State University. He teaches courses in public safety management, contemporary urban issues, and African American images in film. His recent scholarly publications include *Measuring Racial Disparities in Traffic Ticketing within Large Urban Jurisdictions*, which was published in *Public Performance and Management Review* (June 2009) and *Race and the Relevance of Citizen Complaints Against the Police,* which appears in *Administrative Theory & Praxis* (December 2010).

Wornie Reed, Ph. D., is professor of sociology and Africana studies and director of the Center for Race and Social Policy Research at Virginia Tech University. He teaches courses in health and medical care, criminal justice, and Africana studies. Among the other books he has written or edited are *The Education of African Americans* (C. Willie, A. Garabaldi, and W. Reed, eds., 1991), *Health and Medical Care of African Americans* (W. Reed, 1993), *African Americans: Essential Perspectives* (W. Reed, ed., 1993), and *Blacks in Tennessee* (W. Reed, ed., 2008).

INDEX

Nixon, Richard, 92
No Discrimination Thesis (NDT), 6
Northeast Ohio Areawide Coordinating
    Agency, 46

O

Obama, Barack, first African American
    president, 27
Orshinsky, David, 19

P

Passive representation, 117. *see also* Active
    representation
Patterollers, 12
Petit apartheid, 10
Police abuse
    against blacks, 3
    publicized cases of, 3
Police discretion, 14
    impact on ticketing patterns, 87
    low-visibility decision making, 14
Police training, 92–93
    informal policy of targeting blacks as
        part of, 92–93
    institutions and organizational behavior, 93
    racially biased policing practices as
        institutional standard of practice, 93
Policing, efforts to change, 130–131
Policy recommendations, 111–112
    collecting racial data on tickets
        issued, 111
    enactment of municipal legislation, 111
    police deployment patterns, 111
    racial profiling, 111
    use of technology like cameras, 111
Politicizing, traffic cameras, 123–129
    addressing racial bias in ticketing, 124
    Hawthorne Effects, 127
    layoff of employees, 123
    legislation on racial profiling, 125–127
    placement of cameras, 125
    public perception of traffic cameras as
        cash-cow, 124
    reduced number of police-involved
        shootings, 127
    Traffic Stop Data Collection Project,
        125, 126
    traffic stops and tickets by race, 128
Post-racial America, 27

Post-racialism, 27
Post-traumatic stress disorder (PTSD), 103
    DSM-IV diagnostic criteria for, 103
Powder cocaine, 106
Pretextual traffic stops
    consequences of, 2
    as crime-fighting technique, 2
    ending use of, 4
PTSD. *see* Post-traumatic stress disorder
    (PTSD)
Public policy, study's influence on, 120

R

Race and politics, Cleveland style, 115–120
    active representation, 117
    allocation of seats in City Council, 117
    black empowerment, 116
    black voting, 116
    District Democratic Caucus, 116
    informal policy at City Hall, 116
    passive representation, 117
    21st District Democratic Caucus, 116
    Stokes role in acquiring political
        power, 116
Racial covenants, 13
Racial disparities, 5, 6
    within criminal justice system, 5
    in traffic-ticketing patterns, 41–42
Racially profiled
    prominent African Americans, 29
    Ronnie Dunn, 30–33
Racial profiling
    across race, 29
    act of racism, 96
    approaches to eliminate, 62
    100 cases against professional black
        men, 29
    cases of, 3
    defined, 2
    Harris's research on, 34
    legalization of, 57
    in Ohio, Cleveland, 5
    policies prohibiting, 62
    racial oppression, 28
    Ronnie Dunn's encounter, 30–33
    shift of focus on people of Arab, 5
    statistics, 2
    use of force by police, 2, 3
    Wornie Reed's encounter, 29

CPSIA information can be obtained
at www.ICGtesting.com
Printed in the USA
FSHW011438210820
31FS

9 780757 586866